THE POINT
OF CULTURE
Brazil turned upside down

Célio Turino

Edited by Paul Heritage and Rosie Hunter
with Poppy Spowage

Photographs by TT Catalão, Nanan Catalão
and Ratão Diniz

CALOUSTE
GULBENKIAN
FOUNDATION

Published by
Calouste Gulbenkian Foundation
UK Branch
50 Hoxton Square
London N1 6PB
+44 (0)20 7012 1400
info@gulbenkian.org.uk
www.gulbenkian.org.uk

Original edition © 2009 Célio Turino, published by Editora e Livraria Anita Ltda,
www.anitagaribaldi.com.br
English language edition; main text © 2013 Célio Turino; introduction and
afterword © 2013 People's Palace Projects.

Photographs © TT Catalão (TTC) pages 33, 35–8, 40, 45–7, 81–3, 95; Nanan Catalão
(NC) page 34; Ratão Diniz (RD) pages 4, 39, 41–4, 84–94, 96, cover.

Translated by Novas Languages, Paul Heritage and Rosie Hunter.

ISBN: 978-1-903080-18-4

British Library Cataloguing-in-Publication Data
A catalogue record for this book is available from the British Library

Designed by Helen Swansbourne
Printed and bound by CPI Group (UK) Ltd, Croydon, CR0 4YY

Distributed by Central Books Ltd
99 Wallis Road, London E9 5LN
T 0845 458 9911, F 0845 458 9912
orders@centralbooks.com
www.centralbooks.com

Cover: Circus presentation, Rio de Janeiro. Photo: Ratão Diniz

CONTENTS

Célio Turino. Photo: Ratão Diniz

What paradigms must change?

'From structure to flux.
From a state that imposes to a state that disposes.
From a state that concentrates (wealth and information) to a state that releases energies.
From a watertight state to a penetrable state.
From a state that hides to a transparent state.
From a state that controls to a state that trusts.
From a people that pass responsibility to a people who participate.
From distrust to mutual trust, generating responsibility and freedom.
From public policy focused on deficiency to public policy focused on potential.'

Célio Turino, *Ponto de Cultura,* 'Interview in the Mirror'

FOREWORD

What can a programme of local arts initiatives on the other side of the Atlantic tell us? A lot more than you might expect. I first came across *Ponto de Cultura* in Brazil in March 2010 when I participated in *Points of Contact*, a cultural exchange programme for policy makers, funders and artists from Brazil and the UK inspired by it. I found it very engaging in large part because it reflects our interest, at the UK Branch of the Calouste Gulbenkian Foundation, in the arts and culture as a means of empowering people, stimulating 'self esteem in groups that have limited opportunities and few means of asserting their rights'. To use Célio Turino's words, *Ponto de Cultura* demonstrates the power of culture as 'symbol factory', 'as a right and as citizenship' and 'as an economic activity'.

We are also interested at the Foundation in work which creates new, more meaningful or productive paradigms and *Ponto de Cultura* certainly falls into this category. It challenges some of the perceived orthodoxies of public funding for the arts and culture in the UK in a number of important ways:

- rather than set agendas it supported and developed what existed already in communities based on an appreciation of its abundance and richness;
- it refused to define art and culture recognising that local cultural systems, practices and values have enabled communities to remain cohesive in the face of severe social crisis;
- it made no distinction between the arts and crafts, between amateur and professional or between popular culture and 'elite' arts;
- it was based on an understanding of the importance and value of the arts and culture in achieving social transformation.

Brazil is obviously very different from the UK. However, study of programmes which emerge from a different world view can, in some instances, generate significant learning by enabling us to question dominant ways of thinking and acting.

Can we imagine a programme like *Ponto de Cultura* being developed and supported here in the UK? Relatively little public resource is currently dedicated to supporting community-based, community-led activity or 'socially engaged arts' (or arts activity which also has a defined social purpose). Do we need a new paradigm: a new way of thinking about how the arts and culture can create change, leaving to one side the sterile debate about the instrumental and instrinsic value of the arts and instead focusing on its transformative power, its ability to help people dream and imagine and use their skills and talents to create better futures?

We hope that the story of *Ponto de Cultura* will resonate with policy makers and funders and contribute to a new and more focused debate about the real value of art and culture: how it touches and makes a difference in people's lives and innovative ways in which it might be supported and fostered in the future.

Andrew Barnett
Director
Calouste Gulbenkian Foundation UK Branch

Note to the reader

This book has many voices. From centre stage comes the voice of Célio Turino, former Secretary of Cultural Citizenship in the Brazilian Ministry of Culture, who wrote a book in Portuguese called *Ponto de Cultura: o Brasil de baixo para cima*. We have taken that book, translated eleven of its twenty-five original chapters that we thought spoke most powerfully to a UK audience into English, and added our own Introduction and Afterword.

The core of the book, the translation of Célio's text, in itself contains more than one voice. His external voice as policy maker argues persuasively for a revolution in cultural policy relevant to the diverse realities of contemporary Brazil. This 'official voice' is heard alongside Célio's own internal poetic voice as he travels across Brazil – from top to bottom – seeing the impact of the radical changes a government programme can bring in the cultural relationship between state and citizen. At the same time, he presents a chorus of previously unheard voices which have shaped the development of the programme known as *Ponto de Cultura*. The strength of his book reflects the strength of that programme: its recognition of the power of the multiple voices of Brazil.

Some stories have been sacrificed. Readers who want to know more of Célio's personal part in Brazil's struggle for a more representative democracy, his technocratic achievement, or the wider Ministry team, must look to the original.

With the encouragement and support of the Calouste Gulbenkian Foundation UK, we have added English tones to the vocal panoply. Not only have we included our own voices as commentators, we have also drawn attention to the voices of UK arts practitioners who have been in dialogue with Brazilian counterparts on the *Ponto de Cultura* programme. In particular David Slater, Artistic Director of Entelechy Arts, speaks of creative collaboration between eighty-year-olds from London and Londrina and how it has articulated the transformative principles at the heart of this book.

The multivocal text means that the reader will find many deliberate shifts in tone, accent and style. This is not a book that needs to be read in any particular order, nor is there a particular priority of knowledge. The rhetoric of the Brazilian government official and the reflections of UK-based arts practitioners and researchers take their place alongside the song of the indigenous woman.

INTRODUCTION
Brazil turned upside down

In 2009, I introduced a collection of essays called *Intense Dreams* with a general reflection on contemporary Brazilian cultural policy. The opening essay, entitled 'Forgetting Brazil', described to the UK reader the *Cultura Viva* programme and the creation of the *Pontos de Cultura*. A version of that essay follows below. *The Ponto de Cultura* programme was developed by Célio Turino, Secretary of Cultural Citizenship at the Brazilian Ministry of Culture from 2004–10. It has continued to be a focal point of my own research, and of the interest taken by UK cultural policy makers and artists in recent years, as we reflect on what we can learn from Brazil's efforts to define and develop its cultural inheritance and to impact on its social realities through the arts.

The growing interest in Brazil's transformational cultural policies and practices has led to a knowledge-exchange programme inspired by the *Cultura Viva* programme, produced by People's Palace Projects in partnership with Arts Council England, the British Council and Brazil's Ministry of Culture. Now in its fourth year, *Points of Contact* has become part of the British Council's broader cultural exchange programme with Brazil known as *Transform* (2012–16). At the initiative of Calouste Gulbenkian Foundation UK, Rosie Hunter and I have edited and adapted a translation of Célio Turino's eloquent unfolding of the programme's inception and growth, with its original introduction by Emir Sader.

Célio's unmatchable knowledge of the *Pontos*, his delight in the ways that the programme has connected with the lived experience of people across Brazil, are testimony to the rich inspiration that the *Pontos* provide and an insight into how cultural policy can be created in partnership with artists and communities. His book is as much a provocation to think again about the ways in which arts and cultural policy is conceived as it is an insight into the hidden cultural practices of Brazil. In the Afterword, we delineate some of the ways that UK organisations have connected with this inspiration and the paths that their work has taken in collaboration with Brazilian *Pontos*.

Making a point of culture

The *Cultura Viva* – Living Culture – programme, initiated by Gilberto Gil when he became Minister of Culture in 2003, is based on the strong desire to 'unhide Brazil'. But it does not suppose that it can ever be found in a coherent form that will 'explain' itself. By valorising *Pontos de Cultura* – Cultural Points[1] – the emphasis is placed not on single, fixed or unified meanings, but on the journeys that can be made between them. The programme is innovative not just because it has found ways to recognise and fund artistic activities that previously existed outside of public funding mechanisms, but for the way in which it creates bridges and networks between cultural and social initiatives. It is in the veins between the nation's 'vital points'[2] that the programme finds its strengths. Given the colonial histories of Latin America, the *Cultura Viva* programme also offers a challenge to the presumed cultural hierarchies that have privileged other forms over those associated with popular cultural expression. When popular culture has been favoured within the region, it has been within structures that sought to domesticate or pacify[3] anything subversive or politically challenging. The presence of European cultural forms in Latin America is less a result of the Enlightenment than an unacknowledged reminder of the extermination of native peoples and their forms of expression. It would be politically naïve, culturally impossible and wholly inappropriate to create a false rupture with those histories that have contributed to the multiple ways in which Brazil expresses itself. Over five centuries, Brazil has in its own particular ways devoured aesthetic influences from across at least three continents to produce its own distinct forms of cultural expression. The question that faces those creating cultural policy for the twenty-first century is how to respect the multiplicity of those traditions, even where they have created a legacy of inequality and exclusion. How to address cultural imbalances that are also social, while at the same time not betraying the diversity that makes Brazil?

In creating a programme that directs funding towards forms and structures of popular culture, the Ministry of Culture under Gilberto Gil began to reshape or at least re-imagine the Brazilian artistic pyramid that had for so long been constructed according to European cultural and social values. By allowing a high level of self-determination, the

---

1. I am using the translation of the programme titles that the Ministry itself uses when describing the *Cultura Viva* and *Ponto de Cultura* programmes to an English-speaking audience.
2. Gil first invoked the term *pontos* in his inaugural address when he imagined that his Ministry would 'perform a kind of anthropological acupuncture, massaging meridians and spaces which have become temporarily unvalued or dormant in the cultural body of the nation.' See pp. 99–100 of this book; also in *Living Culture* (2005), p. 42.
3. See José Jorge Cavalho, 'Culturas populares: contra a pirâmide de prestígios e por ações afirmativas', in Lima *et al.*, ed. (2005), pp. 34–7.

programme sought to avoid state appropriation of such forms. The aim was that the challenges, the questions and the re-imaginings they offer can reflect those historical and social processes that have enabled them to survive in the face of the forces that have sought to annihilate them. When Gilberto Gil gave a lecture in Germany shortly after announcing the *Cultura Viva* programme in 2004, he defined three dimensions for culture that would give contours to his ministerial actions:

i)   culture as symbol factory;
ii)   culture as a right and as citizenship;
iii) culture as an economic activity.[4]

Describing culture as a nation's factory of symbols, he asked that the actions of his Ministry should be understood as exercises in applied anthropology: 'The Ministry must be like a light that reveals, in both past and present, the things and symbols that make Brazil what it is.'[5]

The *Ponto de Cultura* programme conceived and implemented by Célio Turino can be seen as bringing together all three dimensions of the vocation that Gil described for his Ministry, but its fundamental role has been to shape and fulfil the second category. Gil described *Pontos de Cultura* from the outset as 'sharp interventions into the depths of urban and rural Brazil that aim to awaken, stimulate, and project that which is characteristic and most positive in communities in marginalised societies.'[6] Juca Ferreira, the Executive Secretary at the Ministry of Culture who succeeded Gil as Minister of Culture in 2008, has described how the Ministry has attempted to respond to basic social and political necessities through its policies:

> *'We aim to reposition culture as a right for all Brazilians and as part of strategic public policies for this government in order that Brazil can face up to the challenges of the beginning of the twenty-first century.'*[7]

The Ministry's actions are an attempt to give recognition to a process whereby the absence of the state and appropriate public

4. These three objectives, and the other features of the programme described below, were set out in a series of public announcements of the Ministry of Culture's legislative programme: Decree Nº156, 6 July 2004; Public Announcement Nº1, 16 July 2004; Public Announcement Nº2, 29 March 2005; Public Announcement Nº3, 20 April 2005; Public Announcement Nº4, 20 April 2005. Available on the Ministry of Culture website: www.minc.gov.br
5. Gilberto Gil, 'Experimentation, memory, and invention', inaugural address on being sworn into office as Minister of Culture, Brasília, 2 January 2003, in *Living Culture* (2005), pp. 40–3.
6. Gilberto Gil, 'What happens when you set a bird free?', statement concerning the *Living Culture* programme, Berlin, Germany, 2 November 2004, in *Living Culture* (2005), pp. 8–9.
7. Juca Ferreira, 'Cultura e dignidade do povo brasileiro', in *Prêmio Cultura Viva: a cultura faz o Brasil* (Brasília, Ministry of Culture, June 2006).

policies has been compensated for by community action, NGOs and social movements in the areas of health, education and security. Almost all of these have used culture as a strategy of empowerment, and as an important stimulus of self-esteem in groups that have limited opportunities and few means of asserting their rights. In the face of severe social crises, civic society in Brazil has looked to culture as an important instrument for social cohesion. The *Cultura Viva* programme aimed to identify and train mediators between the state and society, building the cultural capacity of social agents, activists and artists to 'shape rights, behaviours and economics'.[8]

When announcing a competition to reward the many achievements of the first year of the *Ponto de Cultura* programme, the Ministry established a category for what it called *tecnologia social* (social technologies) – recognising the expertise that has been developed in projects that propose creative, participatory solutions to the needs of a local population. Prior to this programme, such initiatives had been developed despite the indifference of the state, rather than because they were valued, supported or encouraged. 'Social technology' is based on stimulating forms of cultural leadership that are autonomous, shared, and transformative. Instead of rejecting art's instrumentalist function – *de rigueur* in contemporary British defences of the arts – the Brazilian Ministry of Culture invoked the technological capabilities of artists engaged in transformative social action. A ministerial promotional document defining the *Cultura Viva* programme cited the Greek mathematician Archimedes' belief that with a lever long enough he could move the world. In creating the *Pontos de Cultura*, Gil and his team, headed by Célio Turino, were not ashamed to think they could build the means to create that leverage.

In 2004, the National Programme of Culture, Education and Citizenship – *Cultura Viva* – launched the first funding scheme to select and support *Pontos de Cultura*. The programme started from the belief that there is an abundance and a richness about Brazilian culture that is independent of the state. Diversity, then, is key to understanding the programme and how it operates: and this is reflected in the structure of Célio's narrative, which encounters and celebrates a series of individual cultural leaders and their *Pontos*.

Diversity is not just a policy requirement from the Ministry, which seeks to manipulate the creation of culture according to a model that reflects current social trends. The recognition that Brazilian culture is

---

8. Célio Turino, 'Unearthing a deep Brazil', in *Living Culture* (2005), p. 14–17.

defined by its diversity is the reason why the *Cultura Viva* programme is based on the stimulation of the *Pontos de Cultura*. Diversity, for Gilberto Gil, is what makes Brazil *Brasil*. The challenge is to create public policy that can maintain, develop and celebrate the 'imperfect mosaic'[9] that is Brazilian culture. Naming and funding the *Pontos de Cultura* has been a way of celebrating and developing that diversity against opposing forces that seek to limit the ways in which Brazil sees and shows itself.

The range of activities undertaken by the *Pontos de Cultura* is thus the most significant feature of the programme. The intention is that the *Ponto* itself chooses, or rather has already chosen, what to do. The approach self-consciously differs from systems by which arts funding bodies usually make decisions, set agendas or monitor achievements. By supporting and developing what exists, and, even more important-ly, by refusing to define what is art and what is not, the state has been able to align itself with forces that are potentially in creative, critical dialogues with what is both local and also tuned to influences from outside. Rather than seeking to shape Brazilian culture, the *Cultura Viva* programme is allowing the processes of existing cultural manifesta-tions to establish new relationships and support emerging identities that are negotiated between the local and the global, the regional and the national, the universal and the particular.

Pontos de Cultura are spread across every region, and can be found on the peripheries of major cities as well as at the centre of remote villages. By August 2007 there were over 600 *Pontos*, and in October the Ministry of Culture announced its intention of creating 3,000 by 2010, with a predicted investment of R$4.7 billion (approximately £1.4 billion). The process continues through a combination of federal, state and municipal funding programmes.

While the averred aim has been to remove the 'arrogance of the state'[10] by recognising the force of what already exists, it is clear that the selection process for the *Pontos de Cultura* has not been neutral or passive. The programme declared its priorities from the outset:

- low-income groups in areas where there is scant provision of public services, both in big cities and in small towns;
- teenagers and young adults who live in socially vulnerable conditions;

---

9. Sérgio Mamberti, Secretary for Identity and Cultural Diversity, Ministry of Culture, 2003–8, 'Brasil, mostra a tua cara!', in Lima *et al.*, ed. (2005), pp. 21–3.

10. The *Pontos de Cultura* were not created in 'laboratories of authoritarian prepotency', Gil, in Araújo, ed. (2006), p. 15.

- students enrolled in state schools;
- those living in regions and municipalities that are highly relevant to the preservation of Brazil's historical, cultural and environmental heritage;
- indigenous, rural and *quilombola* communities;[11]
- cultural agents, artists and producers, teachers and coordinators of primary education, as well as social activists who are carrying out actions aimed at combating social and cultural exclusion.[12]

Resistance is the echo to the rhetoric. Priority is given to those who have learnt to use culture as a means of preserving identities, existence, physical and environmental spaces that are otherwise under threat. The diversity that the programme celebrates and promotes is one born out of the fragmentations created by adversity.

Many of the artistic languages and cultural processes that emerge in these *Pontos* are those that have turned the influences that sought to destroy them into creative forms of expression and being.[13] The ministerial team that created the programme argues through the literature associated with *Cultura Viva* that the maintenance of local cultural systems, practices and values is the means by which communities have resisted the violent consequences of social exclusion for so long. It is the most convincing argument for the direction of new funding to existing projects rather than to new programmes. Arts-based initiatives that attempt to address issues of inequality and injustice have to be based on the recognition and strengthening of the historical reference points that have ensured the resistance that has made survival possible in the extreme cruelties of Brazilian social realities.

The same echoes could be heard when the Ministry of Culture mounted an exhibition of the work produced by the *Pontos de Cultura* in 2006, choosing as a venue the recently inaugurated Museum of Afro-Brazilian Culture in São Paulo. Gilberto Gil emphasised the synchronicity of the museum with the *Ponto de Cultura* programme in the catalogue for the exhibition. The Afro-Brazilian museum aims to 'shine a light on our past, to interrogate ourselves about our society and our culture'.[14] Both Gil and Emanoel Araújo (former Secretary of Culture for the state of São Paulo, creator of the Museum of Afro-Brazilian Culture and curator of this first exhibition of the *Cultura Viva*

---

11. Communities founded by escaped or rebel slaves and now populated by their descendants.
12. *Living Culture* (2005), p. 19. There is a more detailed list of the priority areas for funding in the Ministry of Culture's Public Announcement N°3, 20 April 2005. See www.minc.gov.br
13. See Gil, in Araújo, ed. (2006), pp. 14–17.
14. Gil citing Araújo, in Araújo, ed. (2006).

programme) dismiss notions of popular culture as something that is produced by 'modern primitives' who inhabit a historical cul-de-sac that has lost its connections to the modern world. Célio Turino shares their suspicion of this patronisation of popular forms. Popular culture is seen as a contemporary process, often with traditional roots in the collective memories of excluded communities, which re-imagines everyday lives through artistic practices.

Turino,[15] who as Secretary of Cultural Programmes and Projects and later Secretary of Cultural Citizenship within the Ministry of Culture was responsible for the implementation of the *Cultura Viva* programme, views the healthy development of social relations as being based in the capacity to see ourselves reflected and made manifest in cultural forms. He identifies much of the social violence that Brazil experiences as coming from invisibility: from the denial of the vast majority of the population of the right to see itself reflected in the cultural 'mirror'. He describes the response of his *Ponto de Cultura* programme: the attempt to establish the protagonism of communities in creating those images that are necessary to validate lives that have been destroyed through the exclusion of invisibility.

The multiple ways in which those Brazilian realities are reinvented through cultural manifestations is the basis for the critical enquiry that Turino identifies as one of the clear goals of his programme. It would not, perhaps, be possible to see evidence for critical thinking in each *Ponto*, but the process of exchange that the Ministry promotes ensures that there is a dynamic that goes beyond the moment of each action. And it is important for the *Pontos* to be seen as sites for viewing as well as for being viewed. They need to see what is around them in order for them to be genuinely able to operate in a mode of critical exchange with their own social and cultural realities: 'it is in this exchange, this desire to see and be seen, that a new way of being Brazilian will take root.'[16] The *Pontos de Cultura* address historic and actual absence. They allow Brazilians who daily disappear to become more present for those who actively or otherwise deny their presence.[17]

Although the programme is clearly rooted in the individual *Pontos*, its focus is on constructing bridges and networks. The aim is to create new ways in which culture can circulate and flow through the Brazilian social economy. The Ministry of Culture has regularly staged *Teias* –

---

15. I interviewed Célio Turino at the Ministry of Culture in Brasília on 14 November 2007.
16. Turino, in Araújo, ed. (2006), p. 21.
17. See Gil, in Araújo, ed. (2006), p. 17.

webs – that bring together representatives from hundreds of *Pontos de Cultura* across the country. The image is significant for its suggestion of organic development and lack of vertical hierarchies, although one that still presumes a centre. Perhaps what is important is that the peripheries connect independently but still with access to the centre. The strength is in the structure.

The *Teias* are a way of demonstrating one of the key features of the programme: the stimulation of dialogue through cultural action. Not only is the programme envisaged as a means for strengthening a greater transit of popular culture through mass markets, but it is also predicated on the creation of a different set of symbolic exchanges. The aim is to stimulate new social bonds across Brazil's evident and extreme divisions: economic, geographic, racial, generational, etc. The programme seeks not only to recognise the diversity of Brazil, but to bring various Brazils together in ways that re-evaluate and re-imagine human and economic exchanges.

It is the valorisation of the constant movement and fluid exchange that is seen as being the heart and the heat of the artistic transaction in *Cultura Viva*. Cultural processes and manifestations are brought into an economy that often only finds ways to value products and goods. This is vital if Brazil is to give symbolic value to a patrimony not based on material yield. Cross-cutting the talk of the symbolic and the intangible is always the promise of the delivery of social development goals defined on other ministerial agendas in Lula's, and now Dilma Rousseff's, government. It is noticeable that the language used in the Ministry of Culture's literature that accompanied the programme has often been medical. Social divisions are 'wounds', culture 'heals' and it is the artist rather than the state that is the potential 'healer'. The actions are symbolic, but corporeal, and seek a signification in the real. The location of the *Pontos de Cultura* in the 'real world' is perhaps one of their defining features, and marks them out from forms of traditional 'elite' culture that have often struggled to establish their links outside their fictive practices.

Emanoel Araújo has emphasised repeatedly that one of the most important features of the Ministry of Culture's initiative is not the way popular and elite cultures are seen as distinct but how the *Pontos de Cultura* blur distinctions. Before even considering the fusion or the flux that this programme seeks to achieve between popular and erudite or elite, it is necessary to recognise that popular culture is understood in Brazil as both a distinct set of practices and a conceptual embrace between artistic endeavour and everyday life. Although the pottery, sculpture, embroidery, literature, dances, wood cuts and paintings associated with Brazilian Popular Culture could perhaps be translated into English as 'craft work' or 'folklore', this would in no way do justice to the force of the phenomenon. It shares many features that are often associated with European craft traditions, being based in traditional activities, rooted in local sites of production, and maintaining a certain anonymity for the artist or artisan who excels in repeating methods that have been passed down rather than striving for original or innovatory interpretations of reality. But Brazilian Popular Culture is a vital part of the active expression of contemporary Brazil. It extends to so much more than the traditions that Britain and other countries have come to see as 'folkloric', with the echoing sense of loss that comes with the concept. It has been evoked by academics and artists throughout the twentieth century as providing an 'authentic link' to the ways in which the poorest – and most populous – communities of Brazil think, feel and react. As such it is subject to all the vagaries of interpretation, idealisation and appropriation that come with the different political and aesthetic movements that have sought to preserve and promote its values and forms. Nor is it necessarily helpful to speak of popular culture in the singular rather than the plural, as the phrase can reduce practices that are more prolific and varied than the portfolio of any European public arts agency.

This current initiative from the Ministry of Culture has ideological links to movements in the twentieth century that have sought to 'rescue' forms of expression that are marginalised by the mass media that is seen to serve particular political interests. In a country that is the size of continental Europe, one television company can regularly ensure that 70 per cent of Brazil's television sets are tuned to its daily diet of soap operas, popular journalism and light entertainment. *TV Globo* is the fourth largest private television company in the world, and it has successfully created national cultural reference points that seemingly cross all the geographical, social and ethnic divides of 185 million people.[18] *'Globo e Você: A gente se vê pôr aqui'* ('Globo and You: We can all see ourselves here') is just one of many slogans that relentlessly emphasise *TV Globo*'s supposed capacity to reflect Brazil, despite the obvious distance it keeps from the diverse reality of its audience. Brazilian *Cultura Popular* is the antithesis to Mass Culture; its preservation is a form of resistance to the homogenising effects of globalisation.

---

18. The statistics given here have not been updated in adapting the 2009 essay for the current context; they are contemporary with information quoted in Célio Turino's book.

Any attempt to link popular culture to the apparatus of the state, however well-intentioned, will obviously bring the inherent threat of extinguishing the very essence that the initiative seeks to preserve. In a neo-liberal social democratic state, the market will inevitably be invoked as part of the means by which any initiative is sustained. The Ministry of Culture set out a path for supporting Brazilian Popular Culture that reflected the pioneering educational and political agenda of President Lula's government, as well as its faith in the capitalist economic model as a means for development. The incorporation into the state is thus also a recognition of the role that the market should play in any contemporary cultural forms. The very fact that most of these 'genuine' popular manifestations are linked to forms of poverty and marginalisation means that they are most vulnerable to a political and commercial domination that seems to threaten the basis for which they are invoked. The greater the distance travelled between necessity and excess, the more a practice may be scrutinised for its supposed failure to achieve authenticity. Rio de Janeiro's *samba* schools, which 'produce' the most famous manifestation of the city's annual carnival, are perhaps the most obvious examples of the gap that is seen to open between the popular and the productive.

The sense of danger to these forms seems heightened by the extinction of so many of the traditions in Europe, especially when the majority of the performance manifestations have origins in the culture of Catholicism, which is itself under threat. The dance-dramas associated with religious and secular rural cycles are an intrinsic part of what is recognised as Brazilian Popular Culture: *maracatu, bumba-meu-boi, cavalo-marinho, quadrilha, Festa do Divino, Folia de Reis, caboclinho,* etc. Performed annually at *festas,* usually associated with specific parts of the Catholic Church's calendar, they involve elaborate costumes, often created collectively in communities that observe an annual rhythm. There are three distinct cycles of performance: *Ciclo Natalino, Carnaval* and *Ciclo Juninho.* The first cycle includes the dances and performance rites associated with Christmas, the second marks the activities associated with Carnival (the four days before Lent[19]), and the final cycle commemorates the three saints' days that fall close together at the end of June: Saint Anthony, Saint Peter and Saint John. Each has a different set of dances, performances, costumes, rites, behaviours, etc. These are so distinct in some parts of the country that it is possible for the Secretary of Culture in Recife, a city in the

---

19. The date of Carnival changes each year with those of Easter and Lent.

Northeast, to go on stage on 6 January[20] and announce the end of the *Ciclo Natalino* and the beginning of *Carnaval*. As her words float across the thousands gathered in the city's central square for the annual *Queima da Lapinha* – the ritualistic incineration of the nativity scenes that have decorated the city for the last six weeks – the band strikes up the rhythms of *frevo*. It is time for a new dance to begin. The Secretary of Culture ends her speech, which has involved prize giving for the best artists of the *Ciclo Natalino*, with the simple shout of *'Viva Cultura Popular!'* Taken up by the crowd that spills out of the cobbled square in front of the sixteenth-century cathedral, the night air throbs with the cry of 'Long live Popular Culture!' as the ashes from the burning nativity scenes fall across the manic *frevo* dancers that have emerged to take centre stage.

From Salvador in Bahia up to São Luis in Maranhão, the Northeast of Brazil is the area that most fiercely preserves the traditions of popular culture: hence the frequency with which Turino's narrative returns to Northeastern cities and regions. But there is no part of Brazil that is immune to popular cultural influences. Carnival is celebrated at the Iguaçu Falls on the Argentinian border, in Germanic-looking towns in the mountains of the South, through the industrial heartland of São Paulo and on the central highway that cuts through the modernist capital of Brasília. Both the other popular cultural cycles can be experienced in different ways and with different nuances and intensities across the country. Visit any school, factory, prison or even the presidential palace in June and experience the nostalgic and often comic invocation of a rural wedding in the dance of the *quadrilha*. Brazil is not a simple division of regions. They fold into each other, as country merges with city, and in the flux of cultures no centre holds.

The Northeast is marked out as Brazil's poorest region by the most brutal of socio-economic indicators. It is therefore the source of most internal migration, hence the spread across Brazil of many of the popular cultural practices that still bear the mark of the Northeast. It is possible to find *maracatu* and *cavalo-marinho* in the *favelas*[21] in Rio de Janeiro and São Paulo. Meanwhile the Northeastern rhythm of *forró*[22] has become part of the pulse of Brazil, just as *samba* emerged

---

20. Epiphany – The Feast of the Kings – in the Christian calendar.
21. Shantytowns.
22. Not so much a Northeastern dance-drama, as a type of music. It supposedly originates from the dances of rural workers who, excluded from grand balls, would dance outside the venue, until that moment when the dance became 'for all'. Hence, *forró*. In recent years, it has been mixed with other urban dance rhythms to make a particularly Brazilian form of contemporary dance club music that can be heard across the country.

from the *carioca*[23] hillsides eighty years ago to become the nation's heartbeat. As popular culture is located in the everyday rhythms of life, it is made manifest as much in food, clothes, stories and religious practices as it is in dance, drama, literature, and painting (all of which are directly influenced within these traditions by the experience of the everyday[24]). Thus popular culture has been borne in recipes and games and spiritual beliefs as much as in the formulations of formal artistic activities. The Afro-Brazilian religion of *candomblé,* the martial and magnificent art of *capoeira* that slaves developed as an almost-dance, the taste of *dendé* oil in a *moqueca* (fish stew), each embed cultural memories within the collective identity of Brazil.

The social network and community organisation that makes such activities possible predate any ministerial programme and, it is to be hoped, will survive its eventual demise or transformation. *Cultura Viva's* strength is that it recognises its own impermanence and super-ficiality in relation to the forces that can, for example, bring a seventeen-year-old *maracatu* participant to sew sequins onto his group's costumes every afternoon alongside his father for four months of each year. The ministerial team responsible for the programme invokes its transactional nature across different areas of state inter-vention, but many of the activities supported by *Pontos de Cultura* are in areas where, prior to 2003, government initiatives in health, educa-tion, security, sanitation, housing and employment had been scarce or non-existent. The state arrives with financial investment in cultural activities. New social values are conferred by the state in a context where they have been historically absent, and have yet to find an appropriate agency. The Ministry of Culture's programme professes a desire to enhance communication between different world views, but there is an unsettling disparity to the perspectives. The visibility of one state sector hardly seems to balance the obscurity in which com-munities remain for other parts of the government. Célio Turino is anxious not to make false attempts to furnish the *Pontos* with a functionality in terms of wider state agendas, and the ministerial team has always been vague about their desire to see their financial viability

---

23. Describing that which comes from or belongs to Rio de Janeiro.
24. The best teacher of *samba* I have seen is the one who taught the stiff and rigid bodies of the *gringo* to imagine coming down the *favela* hillside in a drunken stagger. Somehow this image seems to allow the impossible off-beats of the rhythm to arrive naturally in the feet of even the most resistant European. The links between the physicality of everyday – like the tasks and work of the country, the *favela,* the home – can be seen throughout all forms of sculpture, painting, dance, theatre and literature in Brazilian Popular Culture.

in terms of the market. They chose to value a notion of autonomy as a way of recognising the importance of individual and collective protagonism as an indicator of the original and ongoing success of each of the *Pontos*. Thus, artists and arts organisations are encouraged to deliver according to their own agendas, and maintain whatever was their original generative spirit. If *Cultura Viva* is to have a purpose, it is seen to be in its capacity to increase the potential for these *Pontos* to be powerful agents within their own spheres, as defined on their own terms. The denial of a more active agency for the state is almost inherent in the programme. Given the failure of the state in other ways within most of the communities this programme serves, this produces an ambivalent tension between interventionism and protagonism, between rights and responsibilities.

Turino emphasises the transversality of cultural action and the sharing of the management and shaping of the *Pontos de Cultura* between public authorities and the communities of participants, users, artists and other social agents. The *Ponto de Cultura* programme is a conscious effort to build a stronger 'social capital' in Brazil, which envisages a role for public policies and government that does not look to control but to facilitate the demands of civil society. It recognises that any effective response to the current Brazilian crises will ultimately depend on the rebuilding of social relations by, with and within the very communities that are devastated by the extremes of poverty and violence. By investing in the *Pontos*, which are already embedded in the fabric of those communities, there is perhaps the chance to generate the social capital needed for such reconstruction.

When the Ministry of Culture used the name *Cultura Viva* for their programme they were paying tribute to those traditions which still develop artists today, and where artistic activities are an important part of people's everyday lives, ways of being and means of expression. The programmes developed under this policy look to cultural manifestations as living action, as a set of identifiable social and political practices and as a civic right. What is significant is that the programme has refused to observe the distinctions between popular and erudite that have previously been so carefully demarcated in ministerial actions as well as in general cultural assumptions in Brazil. The exhibition that Araújo mounted at the Museum of Afro-Brazilian Culture respected this flux that the *Pontos* themselves aim for, where there are no established limits between established professional 'high' arts practices and those associated with popular traditions.

Too early …?

'It is still too early to evaluate the impact of the Pontos de Cultura from the perspective of tangible results or outputs that attract the eyes of the consumer or the market. It is still too early to perceive the level of autonomy that has been stirred up in thousands of people, in hundreds of groups. It is still too early for conclusive reports about the targets reached when we are implementing a Programme that has as its roots the commitment to a living culture.' [25]

Gilberto Gil resisted a conclusion about what had been achieved through the *Ponto de Cultura* programme. Turino echoes Gil's resistance in this book, but at the same time implies that the rationale that usually makes such assessments is itself limited and inadequate. Rather he asks us to try to understand and identify the *Pontos* 'without norms, central directives or single pathways. Let the *Pontos* grow, integrate, exchange experiences, overcome challenges, choose their own way.'[26] Perhaps that is how British artists, audiences and policy makers can best engage with the arts and cultural initiatives that continue to grow from Brazil's Living Culture.

June 2013: as we finish editing the translation, Brazil is being turned upside down by daily street demonstrations. Events will have moved on by the time this book is published, but Turino's vision of Brazil being recreated from the bottom to the top has become that much more resonant. We hope that the echo of his writings, the policies he implemented and their continuing legacy will also find resonance for any reader who seeks to go beyond an understanding of what makes the *Pontos de Cultura* Brazilian, to be a reminder and a questioning of what it is to make art.

Paul Heritage

---

25. Gil, in Araújo, ed. (2006), p. 17.
26. Turino, on p. 30 of this book and in Araújo, ed. (2006), p. 24.

Bibliography

Emanoel Araújo, ed., *Viva Cultura Viva do Povo Brasileiro*, exhibition catalogue (São Paulo, Museu AfroBrasil, 2006).

Paul Heritage, *Intense Dreams: Reflections on Brazilian Culture and Performance* (London, People's Palace Projects, 2009).

Ricardo Lima *et al.*, ed., papers from the *Seminário Nacional de Políticas Públicas para as Culturas Populares* (Brasília, Ministry of Culture, 2005).

João Cezar de Castro Rocha (State University of Rio de Janeiro), 'Brazil as Exposition', lecture delivered at the Colloquium 'Grand Expositions', Yale University, October 2001. http://www.lehman.cuny.edu/ciberletras /v08/rocha.html#1 (accessed 12 November 2007).

Secretariat of Cultural Programmes and Projects, *Living Culture: National Program of Art, Education, Citizenship and Solidary Economy*, trans. Andrew Miccolis and Graham Howells, 3rd edn (Brasília, Ministry of Culture, 2005).

JOURNEY TO A 'DE-SILENCED' BRAZIL

In 1991, Brazil passed a law allowing individual and corporate tax-payers to choose to dedicate a percentage of their income tax liability to sponsor eligible cultural projects. Commonly known by the name of the Federal Secretary of Culture who created it, the Rouanet Law raised millions of *reais* of funding for cultural production but meant the withdrawal of the state from its role in encouraging the creation of, and access to, culture. The power to determine public resources was left in the hands of individuals: serving the interests of private businesspeople.

A proliferation of erotic-sentimental theatre productions resulted, starring a couple of actors from the cast of some successful soap opera on *TV Globo*. Financed with taxes not paid to the state, they all promoted the brand images of businesses – banks, telephone companies, etc. Thus a law that was intended to stimulate national culture was co-opted into the marketing strategies of large private companies, at zero cost to them and enormous damage to the resources available for state social and cultural policies.

Culture became a prime victim of globalisation; the commodification of the world invading the cultural sphere in devastating fashion. From infinite diversity, Brazilian culture was reduced to the clichés of soap operas. Brazil was reconstructed in the national imagination by television. Cultural representation dwindled to three or four chic districts of São Paulo and Rio de Janeiro, with a few scenes from the country's folklore thrown in (for export). The absence of the rich diversity of Brazilian people in the nation's history and imagination was thus consolidated.

Luiz Inácio Lula da Silva from the Workers' Party (PT) was inaugurated as President of Brazil on 1 January 2003, with a clear mandate to create a radical alternative to his social democrat predecessor. Bold, imaginative social assistance programmes such as *Bolsa Família* and the hunger eradication initiative *Fome Zero* were matched by similarly audacious and ground-breaking cultural programmes. One of the most innovative, wide-reaching and long-lasting achievements of Lula's government has been the *Cultura Viva*/Living Culture programme which brought into being the *Pontos de Cultura*: points, places and practices of culture – points of life, points where the people have been 'de-silenced'.

When Brazillian Minister of Culture Gilberto Gil invited Célio Turino to develop a programme to democratise access to culture, no one could have imagined the extraordinary initiatives that today cross Brazil from one extreme to the other: from the semi-arid *sertão* to the sea, from Amazônia to the fertile lowlands of the South. The *Ponto de Cultura* programme has provided instruments for the multiple voices of a diverse nation to find expression in music, literature, poetry – it is a programme through which the irreplaceable wealth of our people is demonstrated in daily life.

Turino's book is a map of living Brazilian Popular Culture, disseminated to every corner of a nation that is finally seeking to be a country for everyone. The *Pontos de Cultura* are the *Bolsa Família* of the identities, values, meanings and creative imagination of those who are the majority of the population, but who had become a silent minority.

In this beautiful book – I cannot resist using the word beautiful, beauty is the best way of defining it – Célio Turino shows how his path has become intertwined with the quest for democratic and popular cultural policies for Brazil. In a generation that fought against the dictatorship, the struggle for democracy has continued through the opening up of new paths: in social and cultural democratisation, in creating the means for people to speak, sing, shout, express their dreams and their desires.

By reading this book, you will come to know Brazil, the silenced Brazil, the Brazil that, in former times, was only invited to spectate on a country invented by the white elite from the South, and which is now forging the spaces and time of its emancipation. Enjoy this new Brazil, which is reclaiming its centuries-old paths; making them into instruments for ownership of the modern nation that is being built.

'Before we are real, we are dreamed,' wrote poet and philosopher Paul Valéry. The *Pontos de Cultura* are points of our dreams that have become reality, through the tenacity and creative imagination of people like Célio Turino.

Emir Sader
Brazilian sociologist and political scientist

Culture as a Philosophy of Government

'Culture permeates every social action and, as a consequence, all government programmes. *Culture is behaviour, it manifests itself in our smallest daily relationships, and it is how we position ourselves in relation to the world. Groups organising themselves to identify and take over community assets, or founding cooperatives, are cultural agents; our social behaviour in queues, or the way we respond to bad smells, disrespect or humiliations is culture; a population's resistance, its way of facing adversity, is culture; its struggle, individual or collective, is culture. It is through culture that we transcend ourselves, and it is through culture that the challenge to the working classes and civil society of this country will be articulated and delivered, in its critical reflection of their various demands; redefining symbols, ideas, values and behaviours; defining a project of nationhood. Culture can enable a nation to take a leap forward: to rebuild solidarity, to re-appropriate its own memory, and to achieve transformation.*
...

Culture as a philosophy of government generates returns, is inherently progressive, and broadens horizons. Culture gives meaning and coherence to policy programmes and achievements. Culture is the conducting wire that links the rights to health, transport, housing, school, work, with the underlying agenda of citizenship. It is with culture, and culture alone, that we lead our society towards substantive democracy, placing people on the road to human emancipation, advancing our process of civilisation.'

Célio Turino, *Ponto de Cultura*, 'A Transformative Cultural Policy'

1. THE SILENCED WANT TO BE SEEN AND MAKE THEMSELVES HEARD

Araripe is a plateau that was created when the continents of South America and Africa first separated. The sea-bed reveals fossils of fish from salt-water lagoons found only in the semi-arid *sertão* of Northeast Brazil, and on the African coast of Gabon. It is a plateau of reddened sandstone and green vegetation, in the valley where the sea became the dryland of the *sertão* – the magic *sertão*, with springs, fossils of pterosaurs and dragonflies.

The *sertão* of Cariri, locked between the states of Ceará, Paraíba, Pernambuco and Piauí, is a solitary, silent place, like the Cariri indigenous peoples that once inhabited its valley. In the Macro-Jê family of languages, Cariri comes from *quiriri*: 'silent'. But this isolated place pulses with culture. Its famous sons define Popular Brazilian Music. Luiz Gonzaga, who combined the Northeastern *baião* tradition with the infectious rhythms of *xote* folk dancing and the defiant spirit of the semi-arid *sertão,* conquered urban Brazil in the 1950s. The poet Antônio Gonçalves da Silva, the 'Patativa [Nightingale] of Assaré' became recognised as the voice of the 'massed poor, with the strength of a giant'. The master leather-worker Expedito of Nova Olinda; the independent publisher Lira Nordestina, specialising in the centuries-old popular form of *cordel* books and woodcuts; Father Cicero, the preacher of religion, social and ecological justice, and his friend the Blessed Zé Lourenço, leader of the Caldeirão religious community that famously resisted slavery in the 1930s … each of them in different ways brought this region into the popular imagination of Brazil.

It is in this valley that the voice of our people makes itself heard in all its diversity. Hidden stories of a Brazil that little perceives itself. Just as silence is not empty, but always heavy with meaning, the Cariri is a good place to begin to speak of the *Pontos de Cultura* and their desire to 'uncover' Brazil. The guiding principle is to believe in people, to empower what already exists, make accords and partnerships with those 'from below'.

The *Ponto de Cultura* programme has no required format for spending the Ministry of Culture's grants, and each *Ponto* defines and develops its own activities. In some, it may be the adaptation of a physical space, in others, buying equipment or – as in the majority –

providing courses, cultural workshops and productions in diverse artistic languages and interpretations of reality. The *Pontos* are varied, some concentrating on theatre, others on dance, or music, which may be classical, popular or a mixture of both. Many are in the big cities, principally in the *favelas* and peripheries, others in small towns, indigenous villages, rural populations, and communities of *quilombolas*, descendants of slaves who escaped from plantations. The only element they all have in common is the multimedia studio: a basic kit for editing audio and video, three computers with free editing software, a digital video camera, sound equipment for recording music and a broadband internet connection.

Pontos de Cultura are spread all over Brazil and have begun to consolidate themselves as public policy. This book seeks to reflect on the significance of this work in which I was involved, body and soul, for five years. The *Ponto de Cultura* programme is more than policy under construction; it is a concept, and perhaps a theory. Here I present what I saw and experienced on more than 600 journeys throughout Brazil. I share what I understand the role of the *Pontos* to be in seeking a living culture for a living Brazil. Above all, the *Pontos* express a wish for things to change, and the perception that things are changing, as those 'from below' will not be governed as before.

The *Pontos de Cultura* activate a process of transformation. They do this by expressing culture in its ethical, aesthetic and economic dimensions. The *Ponto de Cultura* programme cannot be pigeonholed; it is neither classical nor popular; neither can its sphere of action be reduced to the dimension of 'culture and citizenship' or 'culture and social inclusion'. It recognises that popular art goes beyond the worship of the naïve. It seeks to make seeing more sophisticated, hearing more acute; to hear the silence, and see what is not shown.

Pontos de Cultura have things to show, and they want to do this from their own points of view. These are narratives in the voice of those who make the culture, and not from the voice of 'another'. Even when benevolent, supportive or complicit, the voice of 'another' will always be the voice and view of an outsider. Democracy will only exist when we have polyphony. Social groups, any groups, need and want to look at themselves in the mirror and know that the image reflected is the one they want to see and to show. This is what it means to become the protagonist. Much of the social maladjustment and violence that we experience in big cities is the result of the vast majority of the people being prevented from seeing themselves and being seen: not a problem that is restricted to Brazil. The concept of the *Ponto de Cultura* programme is also a step towards discovery, tolerance and mutual respect.

Back to Cariri ...

In Assaré, there is a *Ponto de Cultura* beside the memorial to the poet Patativa. This *Ponto* plans to create a music recording studio and adapt an old auditorium into a cinema club. But keeping culture alive in Assaré or Arapiraca does not only depend on the repetition and/or preservation of Patativa's verses or on the singers of the Arapiraca festival. Keeping culture alive presupposes an understanding that the verses are vibrant and embedded in their world, speaking of the master leathermakers, of the *quadrilhas* in the square which recreate the distant dances of European palaces. The *Ponto* plans to de-silence.

In their commitment to their people, the *Pontos de Cultura* go beyond aesthetics or art to embrace an ethical dimension. Beneath the Araripe plateau lies the small town of Santana do Cariri, which calls itself the 'Paradise of the Flying Dinosaurs'. Araripe Museum (located at Cariri Regional University) is not yet a *Ponto de Cultura*, but has assumed the characteristics of one. The town's prosperity is based on an illegal trade in fossils. Children learn to make plaster replicas, identical to the originals and just as impressive. The replicas are sold, generate income, knowledge; they are palaeontological kits for schools or souvenirs for tourists. There are also mechanical tin dinosaurs made by Maurício Pedreiro, a local artist who once sold tin helicopters and planes at the market. The illegal extraction and smuggling of fossils has been replaced by the creativity of the local people, who can earn a living and help to preserve the vast natural heritage of the planet.

The *Pontos de Cultura* of this region attach value to the artistic production that was already thriving in the Valley of Silence. Lira Nordestina, Brazil's oldest publisher of the oral poetry tradition of the *cordel* that is still in operation, is now a *Ponto de Cultura*. The published *cordel* with its traditional woodcut illustrations also holds silent memories of local histories, such as the brutal massacre and destruction in 1936 of the religious community of Caldeirão, founded by the Blessed Zé Lourenço.

It is still early days to conclude what the *Ponto de Cultura* programme may represent for Brazilian culture. It is better to proceed by identifying it, allowing it to take shape without norms, central directives or single pathways. Let the *Pontos* grow, integrate, exchange experiences, overcome challenges, choose their own way.

There are many *Pontos de Cultura* like those in Cariri.

And there are others very different.

In the state of Rio de Janeiro there is a range of *favela*-based arts organisations such as the internationally renowned *AfroReggae*, the community museum in the Complexo da Maré, *Nós do Morro* theatre group in Vidigal, and *Pontos de Cultura* in communities such as Vila Isabel, Rocinha, Sumaré, Formiga and Mangueira. But there are other types of *Pontos* in Rio: *Casa do Pontal*, which houses Brazil's largest collection of popular art, the traditional popular dance group *Jongo da Serrinha* [Afro-Brazilian musical forerunner of *samba*], a programme for social integration through training in classical music (PIM) in Vassouras, Augusto Boal's Centre for the Theatre of the Oppressed, the legendary street theatre group *Tá na Rua*, and *Me Vê na TV* (See Me on TV).

Meanwhile in the state of São Paulo, the *mocambos* network of descendants of rebelled slaves is a *Ponto*, as is the Society of Observers of Saci [the magical one-legged prankster-child of Afro-Brazilian folklore], and the *caiçaras* (coast dwellers) of Cananeia, the sea folk of São Sebastião, the *Pombas Urbanas* (City Pigeons) Young People's Theatre company in the historic city of Tiradentes, and the country guitar players of *Viola Caipira* Orchestra in Andradina.

In the state of Minas Gerais there are so many *Pontos* because there are so many different Minases, from the Boys of Araçuaí in the Vale do Jequitinhonha, to the puppets of Giramundo.

There are *Cavaleiros de São Jorge* (Knights of St George) in the Chapada dos Veadeiros National Park and the *Mamulengo Presepada* puppet group in the modernist capital city of Brasília. In the Amazon there is a *Ponto* that brings us the musical sounds of the forest (*Som da Floresta*) and another that navigates the river with its TV studio on a boat (*Navegar Amazônia*). The state of Acre has *Pontos* that celebrate the *carimbó* dance of Iaçá and the traditions of the Ashaninka tribe.

The *Pontos* go much further. A hip hop group in Teresina strips down, rebuilds, repairs and repurposes computers to create IT centres in state schools. There are *Pontos* dedicated to animation connecting Olinda to Fortaleza. The *Edisca* dance *Ponto* in Fortaleza works with *Dança Vida* in São Paulo state. There is the *Maracatu* Gold Stars Alliance, Beth de Oxum's *Coco* project in Bahia, the Online Indians, the Alagoan warriors with their *Ponto de Cultura* in the Maceió landfill site, the *Casa da Arte de Dona Edna* for the children of fishermen, the films projected onto the sails of the traditional *jangada* sailing boats, the travelling storytellers of *Griôs* in Lençóis, and the Earth Network of the MST (Landless Workers' Movement) with 200 theatre groups and audiovisual centres.

The *Pontos de Cultura* are many. They are many because Brazil is diverse.

Despite such diversity, much is silenced; *quiriri*. The major media networks and most universities have not yet understood this silent revolution that is sprouting at so many points of Brazil. From time to time news stories highlight the efforts of poor communities to make art, but they do not narrate the emergence of a new social movement, transforming and reinterpreting Brazil. They treat each as an isolated case, led in some instances by an individual artist or community figure, featuring the 'social responsibility' of corporate sponsors, or the efforts of the poor communities. These are conservative interpretations from people who cannot see the real change that is happening. In Heliópolis – the largest *favela* in São Paulo – the community radio station plays a strong role in developing active citizenship and is a *Ponto de Cultura*. With the radio station, residents of the community have managed to bring down rates of violence and catalyse environmental improvements. Their houses and streets have new multicoloured painted façades, and there is a well-stocked community library. The resources to upgrade the radio studio and broadcasting equipment were provided by the *Ponto de Cultura* programme. But the legislation that regulates community radio is restrictive and does not respond to the reality of the communities seeking legitimate self-expression. The concession process for licences takes years, creating a mismatch between the law and the community's desire to break media monopolies. In Heliópolis, as in many places, the people got tired of waiting and started broadcasting. The Federal Police closed them down and seized their equipment. Overlooking the essence of the transformation in progress, the press focused on the contradictions. On the one hand, equipment bought with funding from the Ministry of Culture, empowering polyphony; on the other hand, institutions of the same government cutting off these new voices. The equipment was recovered and a permanent licence obtained. It was a battle with a good result, and the community of Heliópolis could hear itself and be heard.

These are new ways to break the silence and become protagonists, but resistance is a historic movement. The dominant system does not easily accept the emergence of new actors and does everything to eliminate them or, at least, gag them, hide them or subjugate them. Despite the power of those who try to silence them, history follows its course.

The silenced want to be seen and heard, and there will always be points that resist.

Graffito in the
style of a *cordel*
woodcut, on a wall
in Maceió. TTC

PODER DO POVO ESTA NA SUA... ULTURA.

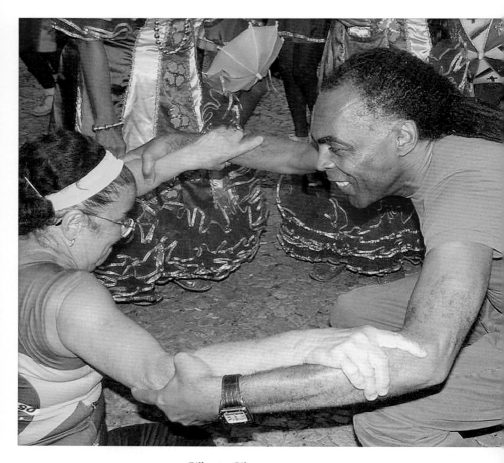

Gilberto Gil
participating in
a *roda de frevo*
(circle dance to a
distinctive *frevo*
rhythm), Recife. NC

Ichaman, a member of
the Yawalapíti indigenous
tribe from Alto Xingu;
graffito at the 2007 *Teia*,
Belo Horizonte
(composite image). TTC

Participant in a *reisado*
group led by *Mestre*
Benon, Alagoas. TTC

Child from *Boi
Juventude* group,
Pirambu, participating in
the closing procession of
the 2008 *Teia*, Brasília.
TTC

A warrior from *Maracatu Rural Estrela de Ouro*, a *Pontão* networking 43 forest-based *maracatus* in Pernambuco. TTC

Graffiti artist Bad Boy and his
artwork at an underground
station in Rio de Janeiro. RD

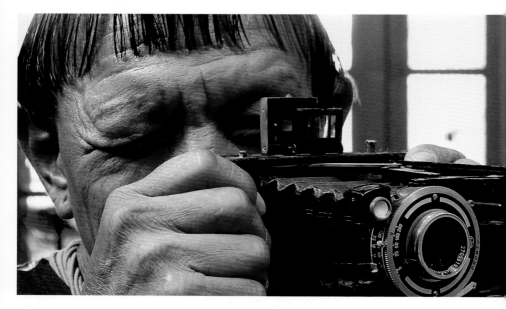

Ichaman, a member of
Yawalapíti *Ponto de
Cultura*, Alto Xingu.
TTC

Young student of
Spectaculu design
and technical school,
Rio de Janeiro. RD

Circus presentation
at a Ministry of
Education seminar,
Rio de Janeiro. RD

*Noite dos Tambores
Silenciosos* (Night of
the Silent Drums),
Carnival Monday,
Recife. RD

Folia de Reis Penitentes
(procession of the Three
Kings), Santa Marta hill
favela, Rio de Janeiro. RD

A Brazilian Indian
visits an exhibition at
the Museu Nacional
da República during
the 2008 *Teia*,
Brasília. TTC

Children of the
Yawalapíti *Ponto de
Cultura*, Alto Xingu. TTC

Boy playing at a state-
sponsored festival of
Pontos, Teresina. TTC

2. THE YAWALAPÍTI
Culture, sustainability and resilience in
a woman's song

In the beginning, the women played the *jacuí* (sacred flute) and sang
for the whole village; the men's role was to listen with reverence. One
day, the men rebelled; they didn't want women at the centre of the
village any longer. They took the sacred flutes and created the *Casa
da Música* (House of Music), built in the *uikúka* (central square). Ever
since, women have been forbidden from playing the *jacuí,* or even
from entering the *Casa da Música,* which has become an environment
restricted to men. But if the men prevented them from playing, they
could not stop them from singing, for they could not steal the voices
from their throats. And thus the women sing.

I was told this story by the *putaki wikiti* (owner of the village,
chief), Aritana, the leader of the Yawalapíti. Son of Kenato, Aritana is
a leader, not only of his people, but also of the many peoples who
inhabit the Xingu National Park, an immense area of 2.6 million
hectares of biological and cultural diversity. Five thousand Indians live
in the Park from fourteen different tribes: Kalapalo, Wauja, Meniako,
Kuikuro, Kamaiurá … various races, linguistic branches, cultures. To
be a leader in the midst of such diversity, one needs to know the
other, be tolerant, learn to listen, speak many languages. Aritana is
polyglot; he speaks eight languages and uses them at the council of
peoples of the Alto Xingu.

The Yawalapíti, whose territory lies between the Tuatuari and
Kuluene rivers, have inhabited the region since time immemorial.
Contact between these tribes and white men was first recorded in
1887, by an expedition led by a German, Karl von den Steinen. The
Yawalapíti are direct descendants of Kuamuti or Mavutsinim, who
planted the trunks of the *Kuarup:* the tree of rebirth. Being born
again from difficulties, even from death itself, was one of the teachings
that Mavutsinim left as his legacy; a teaching that was of great value
when the presence of the white man became more frequent.
Pestilence, viruses and bacteria overran the place and with them
influenza, measles, diarrhoea and infections. Cattle, pasture, soya, meat
production … and with this process came hunger, dirt, and fenced-off
land. Attacks of all kinds, with lethal weapons or with sugar: death,
decay, desperation …

In 1948, there were only twenty-eight Yawalapíti. It was a people under threat of extinction. The solution found by the Villas-Bôas brothers – internationally renowned Brazilian defenders of indigenous rights – and by Kenato, was to bring them together into a single village and form unions with other Xingu peoples. People who had fought among themselves would now have to join together to grow again, as in the *Kuarup* rites. In 2005, there were 230 Yawalapíti, but very few, only five, were fluent in the language and the history of their people.

The peoples of the Xingu may not know the Western laws of physics and the concept of resilience, but they know the teachings of Mavutsinim and the power of the *Kuarup*. Even when subjected to all kinds of strain and adversity, obliged to withdraw, cower, bow down and retreat, their capacity for recovery enabled them to return to their original form and strength. The Yawalapíti are resilient. They are resilient because they perform the *Kuarup*.

For the Yawalapíti to thrive, the great challenge is the recovery of their language. Although the interethnic unions were essential for the rebirth of the Yawalapíti people, the cultural transmission line has been broken.

'You know how it was before, when you arrived in a village. Everyone was painted, everyone very beautiful. It wasn't like today. Before, in the late afternoon, the centre of the village was full of people. Old people, youngsters, boys, all gathered together, talking about what they had done, what they were going to do, telling a story, talking about the day ... today, no, only the elderly go to the centre. It seems that that joy has ended.'
Ichimã Kamayurá

But the roots of the Yawalapíti are strong, they know their stories and they keep them alive in their day-to-day dances and songs.

The Yawalapíti are clever. Among them there is one who has been nicknamed MacGyver by visitors. The scientist of the village, he operates the radio, fixes the car engine, invents things. Their culture is also maintained by invention and by contact with what comes from outside. It recreates itself. Thus they proposed creating a *Ponto de Cultura*.

The concept of the programme is embedded in what their tribe already practised: sharing work and developing cultural activities that respect the autonomy and leading role of communities. As a *Ponto de Cultura* neither creates nor invents itself, but is empowered by what already exists, the idea was easily assimilated. 'The *Ponto de Cultura* is like the trunk of the *Kuarup*', Aritana said.

The Yawalapíti *Ponto de Cultura* activities proposed by IPEAX (Xingu Ethno-Environmental Research Institute) in the indigenous lands of the Xingu include a language school, publication of a Yawalapíti alphabet book, dictionary and grammar, the recording of traditional songs, indigenous performances, Xinguan fashion and body art, crafts, traditional architecture and Yawalapíti on the web. Aritana is president of IPEAX and its board is comprised mainly of indigenous people from the Xingu. The Indians of Brazil have a memory, and they know what happens when they transfer the destiny of their people to others. Even if, in the beginning, the filling in of spreadsheets and the necessary programme bureaucracy seemed difficult for an Indian who lives in Xingu, it is always better that they speak for themselves – without mediation. Outside help, when honest and disinterested, is welcome, but theirs is always the last word. What they need to do, they do for themselves, and thus they gain their autonomy.

In the *Kuarup* in which I participated (in 2007), it wasn't just the elderly that sang the festival repertoire. The repertoire of the Yawalapíti is vast and is becoming lost, and singing a song is not just a case of memorising the words; it is necessary to know the stories, the rites and the emotions. All this is contained within a culture. For ten days a recording and research team followed the dance and musical repertoire of the village. It was a great moment, young people, adults and children exerting themselves so that the language would be fully recorded. But, despite their best efforts, not all the young people were masters of the music.

Suddenly, singing could be heard from inside one of the houses. To everyone's surprise, the voice was coming from the smallest house, the poorest and most forgotten, the least well-maintained. The singing came from the depths of the darkness of the straw house. The old woman Wantsu lived there: one of the five Yawalapíti still fluent in their language. Wantsu sang songs that not even the oldest men remembered. She took them from the depths of her soul, as if from the time when – as well as singing – the women played the *jacuí*.

'*Yamurikumalu*
Ayawa, ayawa rinari
Iyawa riyari Yamurikumari nawikamina
Atsanhia putapa nupikani nukamani
Kamatawira'

'The women warriors
Yamurikumã deserve to be respected
You do not know how I am feeling
And that I will die'

As in the *Kuarup*, the Yawalapíti are reborn. And they come back to life through the singing of a woman. As with the Yawalapíti, Brazilian culture, despite pressure, resists. It is resilient; it finds points of support and leverage. And as it moves, it recreates itself.

3. THE BLUE AND GREEN SEA

'In the middle of the way there was a stone
there was a stone in the middle of the way'
Carlos Drummond de Andrade, *'No meio do caminho'*

As part of the initial process of publicising the funding programme to create the *Pontos de Cultura* across Brazil, I went to Maceió, Alagoas.

I was taken to a hill facing the sea, at the edge of the city.

The blue and green sea.

The coconut trees.

The strong sun.

The beach.

On the hill, stand luxury houses, mansions with a sea view. Above them, vultures.

Rounding the luxury houses, we walked up the hill. I was greeted by a party; a circus band, juggling, clowns on stilts. I followed the band.

Below the hill, the sea.

On one side of the hill, the mansions.

Behind the hill, the village.

Down the hill, a rubbish dump – a vast landfill site.

I understood the vultures.

A strong stench.

A strange noise, a mixture of sounds.

Trucks, birds and people.

Dumping refuse.

Eating refuse.

Fighting over refuse.

The band started to play and march. I had to follow it at quite a pace. A corridor of houses made of wattle and daub. Shacks made of boards, little houses with exposed brickwork, zinc, plastic or asbestos roofs. In front of the houses, people watching the procession pass.

A little girl dressed as a clown on stilts.

I followed the procession watched by the elderly, women and children who were in front of the houses. We arrived. A small house, a room and computers. We went in. Some people were left outside; the house was very small.

The girl on stilts read the letter that the residents would like me to deliver to the President of the Republic:

'*This is where we live. Here we make our living. We have managed to get some taps and electricity, but we want to live better: a crèche for the children, a recycling shed, better houses. Our life is here and we live in hope. The circus came to the village, and the little children can go there. But the older children have to help their parents, finding things in the rubbish dump [she cannot hold back her tears, but continues reading]. We want more time at the circus, more support, more school. We want to rest and make this a good place. This is what we ask of you, Mr President. Help us. Trust in us, because we are Brazilians and we never give up.*'

I can only recall the letter from memory, because on my way back I forwarded it to President Lula.

4. SEA VIEW

In the Northeastern city of Fortaleza they claim that Pirambu is the largest complex of *favelas* in Brazil. Three hundred thousand people – 12 per cent of the population of the city – live on a small strip of earth between the sea and the land. In Brazil, there is always another group of *favelas* disputing the title of the most populous, the most violent, with the most poverty and the highest inequality. But Pirambu has its own history as a site of struggle.

In 1962, when the first shacks were built, there was a small colony of fishermen who welcomed the migrants from the drylands of the *sertão*. Poor folk who worked on the sea together with poor folk from the land. The fishermen had their *jangada* sailing boats but no means to store or distribute their fish, so the kilos of fish that they caught in the early morning were of little value. Over time, they abandoned their fishing. The people who came from the *sertão* had even less, as land is more easily enclosed than the sea, and every square metre of land already had a landlord claiming ownership. Those who arrived in Pirambu hardly had clothing on their backs. They arrived to squalid conditions and without work, because the knowledge that they had learned in the drylands of the *sertão* was worth nothing in the city.

After more than forty years, Pirambu has become a city within the city. Originally distant from the urban centre of Fortaleza, today it practically bumps up against the tourist area but without a beach, promenade or the bustle of tourism. There are no multi-storey apartment buildings or balconies with views of the Atlantic.

Water and land meet in Pirambu, and life buzzes.

Hard work and continual struggle combine with *festa*: the characters of the *bumba-meu-boi* (regional ox dance), the urban *maracatu* (Afro-Brazilian carnival). The songs of the fisherman and the traditions of the dryland *sertão*. Traditions renewed, outbursts recreated in rap, fables performed, modern dances, theatre groups, debating circles, youth groups and popular education. Creation and recreation; earth and water amalgamated; mud, raw ceramics, fired ceramics, porcelain; pure culture.

But a point of support was lacking.

ACARTES, the Academy of Sciences and Arts of Pirambu, may suggest an official, elitist organisation but it is an academy of the people of the *favelas*, 'the largest in Brazil', as suggested in their application to become a *Ponto de Cultura*. Knowledge gained through the experience of life, not at all academic, but in no way less sophisticated and profound. By not getting lost in theories of how and why, the academics of Pirambu have found the essence of life. Writers, poets, playwrights, artists, left-wing militants, cultural agitators, musicians, dancers, designers and graphic artists, inventors, storytellers, masters of *maracatu* and of *boi*, toymakers, playmates and popular artists. Together, they practise the values of hope and solidarity between human beings. All expressed through art. ACARTES is the only cultural facility to which the 300,000 inhabitants of Pirambu can turn.

When I went to Fortaleza to publicise the funding for the *Ponto de Cultura* programme, some academics from ACARTES invited me to visit their *favela*. Damasceno, Cláudia, Raimundo and Juliana were my guides to this vast, densely populated district a few kilometres from Fortaleza's world-famous beaches. ACARTES is run from a little yellow house, very narrow, with a side corridor, two rooms, a kitchen and a bathroom. In the main room, an art gallery and chairs for meetings. In the next room, a community library with well-worn and well-read books: Brazilian and foreign literature, an old edition of an encyclo-paedia, some textbooks and technical manuals, history books, Marxism and philosophy. At the back, a fifteen-metre-long yard used for artistic performances, rehearsals and larger meetings. I remember that at the end of the visit, I said to my hosts: 'When I conceived the *Pontos de Cultura*, I imagined a little house like this.'

Another visit to Fortaleza and to Pirambu. Almost a year had passed. The proposal for the *Ponto de Cultura* had been approved and implemented. The little yellow house was still there with its narrow rooms. A roof had been put up in the backyard to cover a temporary stage and part of the audience, so that some of the chairs were in the open air, allowing the small theatre to receive natural ventilation. A group of young people participated in cultural work-shops; in the library, others were discussing a play; in the backyard, a theoretical class on woodwork and mechanics.

Another year. Another visit.

A new storey had been built above the theatre, with a rehearsal room, computers and a multimedia studio with emphasis on audiovisual production (TV sets, an editing desk and cameras); purchased partly through the Ministry of Culture, partly through donations. At the back, a space that appeared to be a store of old machines and scrap metal. Damasceno said that it would be the production workshop for the theatre and cinema, 'the dream factory'. The apparent disparity between woodwork, mechanics and drama began to make sense.

New resources, new problems, new solutions.

The state is not well set up to have a direct relationship with ordinary people. Bureaucracy is a necessity, but our laws date from a time when the majority of society was excluded from exercising citizenship. The legal and bureaucratic maze generated – and still generates – enormous instability. The group struggles to present its accounts; there have been problems with the payment of scholarships for young people, and resources have arrived late.

Despite being a people shaped by struggle and which has learned that unity is essential for ensuring victory, there are many internal conflicts in Pirambu, as in every community movement. The *Ponto de Cultura* upset the political order of the *favela*: residents' associations, council committees, NGOs, churches, the Catholics, the Evangelists, the football teams … Everyone disputing territory among themselves. Before, ACARTES was only a group of well-intentioned artists, but with no real power. The arrival of a new actor on the stage is never easy.

The delays in payment of agreed funds or in the direct payment of scholarships to young people crush expectations, interrupt the work-flow, cause frustration. Those who feel they are losing their place take advantage of the situation. 'I told you so', 'A flash in the pan', 'Typical of artists', the pessimists said. Others, for whom political space was a question of survival – personal, financial, idealistic – went further: 'I knew they were embezzling money, they all do it.' Good public policy began to fade in the entanglements of bureaucracy.

Meanwhile …

Discussions at the Ministry of Culture in Brasília were divorced from this reality, lost in interminable meetings which either put off the decision until another meeting or invented new rules, rendering problem-solving even more difficult. All of the terms and conditions of the agreement (more than 600 at the time) had to be revised.

But the people of the land and the sea do not give up easily.

Leading the *Ponto de Cultura* there are people like Damasceno. They are people who make the world go round and succeed in their efforts because they rely on the trust of their own community. Gerardo Damasceno was born in Pirambu. The son of a midwife, he roamed its streets and alleyways, was an apprentice printer, then master, progressing to president of the Printers' Union of Fortaleza before studying to be a teacher. Everything he has learned and achieved has been for his people, creating a strong set of bonds. To leave would mean condemning himself to breaking these ties.

When there is a crisis of confidence in the relationship between society and government, public managers need to recognise that they are there to serve the public and not be served by the public.

Something new is happening: the people see themselves as subjects and want to be treated as such.

Another meeting in Pirambu.

I spoke directly to cultural leaders of the community, to young people and to their parents. We signed commitments based on trust. The government establishing direct commitments with the people, without intermediaries, children of country folk and fishermen, people hewn from adversity, who do not falter and know where they want to go. And the work continues.

Sometimes Damasceno sends news of young people who have given up taking drugs or have managed to find work, of a girl who started university, of talented actors who are emerging, of the founder of the group and the new gadgets he has invented. But of all the stories, the one he repeats most often is that of the old resident who went to thank the *Ponto de Cultura* for having got Pirambu 'off the crime page to become news in the culture supplements'. Each victory is shared and celebrated by everyone.

The 'Dream Factory' has become a community enterprise. The heap of metal which had attracted my attention when I saw it piled up at the back of the room started moving, becoming animated puppets, living masks with special effects for the cinema. They also built a perfect mini crane, with a track, lever, counterweight and strap for holding and moving the video camera, like those we see in the making of Hollywood films. It cost R$2,800 (£825): five times less than one made in Brazil, and many more times less than an imported one. They have already received eight orders, all from *Pontos de Cultura* led by people like Damasceno and for people like those of Pirambu.

In Itatinga, a town in the metropolitan area of Fortaleza, they are making their own film set of a city with the support of the local council. Collaborative work, just as they created their *favelas*. Each one gives a little of what they know, offers their art: engravers, bricklayers, carpenters, designers, inventors, woodworkers, artists, mechanics, pavers, poets. These people broaden their own horizons and have been doing so for a long time. When they reach the horizon that is within view, they want to go further.

Cultura Viva is an endless endeavour. As it flows, it spins a web of relationships, solving problems, creating new questions, new solutions and new problems. The objective is to find the essence in different forms and their intentionality. This expresses the sense of the programme: an 'immanent flow of experiences that constitute consciousness', seeking to find out and capture the meaning of things. The quest is for the moment of transcendence, or awareness, or overcoming alienation, or emancipation.

From 2008, the selection or renewal of *Pontos de Cultura* began to be decentralised, incorporating state governments and municipal councils from the largest cities. This new phase broadened and decentralised the programme so that by 2010 there were 3,000 *Pontos de Cultura*. In this phase, there was a risk of conceptual misunderstandings, political co-opting, new and localised management problems, the temptation to control and pigeonhole the *Pontos* into one single form, and a mere transfer of resources to micropower structures. How can this be avoided? There are no answers, but some clues: a lot of autonomy, trusting and believing in people, giving up control, courageously 'throwing oneself into the river' ...

Where do we want to get to? It doesn't matter: when the horizon is reached, we go beyond. That is what I discovered on yet another visit to Pirambu.

Another surprise.

The little house was still yellow (newly painted) and receiving the people into its art gallery, its library, its theatre in the yard (now with sound and lighting equipment), its studio and machinery workshop: the Dream Factory. Above them, a pre-cast concrete circular staircase, simple and narrow.

Eduardo Galeano, author of *Open Veins of Latin America*, makes an analogy between the horizon and utopia in these times of pragmatism and absurdity. Utopia, like the horizon, is always ahead of us, we take some steps and the horizon moves forward, we walk on and the horizon looks further away. 'What is the horizon for, then?' he asks. So that we start to move. The horizon/utopia encourages us to walk.

I went upstairs.

Some steps and living quarters to accommodate workshop leaders and staff.

Another flight of stairs.

I go up and arrive at a covered gazebo, small, but big enough to set up a hammock, lie in the shade and feel the previously hidden sea breeze.

On my previous visits I had not perceived that Pirambu had a sea view from which the horizon could be seen.

5. DARLENE

Red earth in a neighbourhood a long way from the skyscrapers of Londrina, a major city of the state of Paraná.

'From my own kids I realised that we needed something to occupy the children in the community....' Darlene Kopinski proposes the occupation of an abandoned public building. A cultural centre emerges on the outskirts of the city. 'It's open access. If the adults can't come, the children get the key and open the place themselves.'

Jéssica, a fifteen-year-old girl with a gentle manner:

'I do percussion, dance, theatre ... I was working hard and my mother said "I'm going to take her to the centre" – I've done *sambateado*, belly dancing, crochet, *samba*, theatre; I've done a lot of percussion, various things. I've been here for years.'

Darlene is proud of the multimedia studio that she has just received as part of the *Ponto de Cultura* programme. 'Here's where we produce our films and songs.' Open-source software, animation on sheets of A4, drawings that gain movement from the rapid flicking of the little paper book.

A girl with afro hair:

'I came to a class and I liked it ... and I started to participate ... I like dancing; I think it's the only thing I like doing.'

And another:

'I used to leave school and stay out on the streets, I didn't want to do anything else, now I want to come here.'

Paulo:

'I used to live on the streets. Then I wanted to dance, every day, and I wanted to study too ... I didn't know my father very well. All I knew was that he'd got out of prison and that he taught dance.'

With her calm manner and serene gaze, Darlene talks about the results of the *Ponto*'s work: 'After I came to the *Ponto*, we managed to rescue many adolescents from involvement in drugs, serious family conflicts, young people who were depressed, who didn't leave their rooms....'

Edio, a man who does not hide his history, adds: 'We can't prevent anybody from tripping up, but we can offer advice.'

I discover that Paulo is Edio's son:

'Now I'm studying to be an events producer and dance teacher. I'm already a monitor at the *Ponto*,' says the boy, under the proud gaze of his father.

Jéssica interrupts and reveals her dream:

'I want to become a cultural producer. I don't know if it'll be possible, I'm battling for it, we'll see, won't we?'

6. PIAUÍ

Another working visit: destination Piauí.

A quick trip, like so many others: arrive on Friday and return on Saturday, staying little more than twenty-four hours in Teresina, capital city of the state of Piauí.

To the surprise of the audience and the press, at the public presentation about the programme I hardly mentioned the R$14.5 million that would be invested by the Ministry of Culture in the selection of 80 new *Pontos de Cultura*. This money was not a gift to the state. What was more important was to recognise that the decentralisation of the programme via partnerships with the states was only possible thanks to the pioneering experience of Piauí, which in 2005 started its own network with 17 *Pontos de Cultura*. Another surprise; I praised the quality of education in the state. In 2007, the best-positioned Brazilian school in the National Secondary Education Examination – ENEM – was from Piauí. And this was not an isolated instance. Among the projects entered in the *Cultura Viva* awards, a state school from Piauí won first prize. A rural school from the town of Boquinha presented the most consistent pedagogical proposal for the integration of culture in activities in the school and the local community.

It was a fruitful debate.

Some spoke proudly about the best school in Brazil, Dom Barreto, in Teresina, at which various people present had studied. A teacher from Boquinha said that he had been waiting for years for their work to be recognised, and that the *Cultura Viva* award had brought new life to that and other rural communities in the state, many of them with equally daring and innovative experiences. High-quality videos made by young people at local *Pontos de Cultura* are broadcast on the state TV networks. The state of Piauí and its capital have been gaining definition:

'Teresina:
Absence
of a presence …
presence
of the same absence …
only memory in memory
always alive,

only longing … only distance …
only desire.'
Poem by Torquato Neto

We spoke about contemporary artistic languages, about the cave paintings of the Serra da Capivara inspiring the new state logo of Piauí, about the nationally revered poet–journalist Torquato Neto and his influence on the 1960s art movement *'Tropicalismo'*. Invention, tradition and rupture, a *Geleia Geral* (General Mash-up), in which:

'A poet unfurls the flag
and the tropical morning begins.'
Gilberto Gil, *Geleia Geral*

Piauí, a 'pile of concrete, *tropicália*, bananas in the wind'.

Afterwards there was a visit to the *Centro de Criação* (Centre of Creation) of Dirceu, in a poor neighbourhood of Teresina. A collective of contemporary artists who calculate that Art = Thought + Action. I was curious as there has been a generalisation about the *Ponto de Cultura* programme's association only with popular culture and socio-educational initiatives for children and young people from the poor peripherial communities. Yes, the *Ponto de Cultura* programme is this, but it is also classical art, aesthetic research and renewal and everything else that is understood as culture.

Centro de Criação: a collective of eighteen artists with different artistic languages; all practising the cultural 'anthropophagic' movement of the new age. Cannibalistic, devouring and regurgitating in new forms, they are in the vanguard of contemporary art, without becoming removed from the people of Teresina's peripheral communities. They manage a very creditable and well-structured theatre; their activities involve artistic residencies and training audiences. As innovative artists, they know that populism is not the adoption of mass-produced, easily accessible and poor quality art, 'palliative entertainment for desperate social conditions, which patronises and deracinates growth in a society. This misunderstanding of what is popular and accessible ends up stifling any process which enables the education, cultural independence and self-determination of a people.'

Artists of Piauí, Artists of Brazil, Artists of the world, there is no time to lose.

They do it.

I went to find out about the *Ponto de Cultura* of the Organised Hip Hop Movement of Brazil – MHHOB – which takes the name of *Preto Ghoez*. A *Ponto de Cultura* set up in a disused school, sizeable and with decent facilities, with a multimedia studio, recording room (at that time used by 20 bands – 15 hip hop, 3 reggae and 2 rock) and 'meta-recycling' workshops to recover and repurpose scrap computers. They are contracted by the state government to repair 50 computers a month; these computers are given graphite casings and installed in IT suites in state schools, a process of technological empowerment. The *Ponto* also has a community library (50 visits per day), IT centre (250 to 300 users per day), a martial arts room with mats (150 students of karate, 200 of *capoeira*) a dance studio (50 students of street dance), a preparatory course for university entrance examinations (120 students) and community radio, as yet unlicensed, but which reaches a community of 150,000 people.

'See that girl? She travels five kilometres on foot to come to class and uses the R$40 of her government scholarship to help her family. She sells homemade snacks and cakes during the course.' Estânio, history teacher, my colleague, was proud of the determination of those young people. Coordinated by Gil BV, rapper and chemistry student at the Federal University of Piauí, the work of the *Ponto* goes beyond Piauí – they coordinate the national project *Fome de Livro na Quebrada* [roughly translated as: 'hunger for books in peripheral communities'].

During a short visit I saw many things in Piauí. Above all, that the open-source movement in the vanguard of digital culture is akin to the thoughts and deeds of traditional culture, where knowledge and natural resources are universally shared. Traditional festivals and Creole roots come together with open-source software, from medicinal tea to the source code of a computer. Their essence is the same.

The main reason for my trip was to participate in the final class of the opening semester of the Bachelor of Arts degree for members of the agrarian reform movement. This initiative of the Federal University of Piauí, the Ministry of Agricultural Development and the Landless Workers' Movement (MST) provides undergraduate education for sixty rural workers or children of rural workers. First they study land rights, then machinery, training, access to financing, and production flow. But if this structure is not accompanied by a change in their horizon by good educational and culture practices it will do little good. In Piauí, I met the 'landless workers' studying art and wanting more.

The land of the poet–journalist Torquato Neto.

During the debate with the university students from the Landless Workers' Movement, I was asked an unexpected question. They asked me to make a parallel between the principles that we adopted with our Digital Culture programme, and the struggle for food sovereignty. I replied:

Humanity made us what we are – *Homo sapiens sapiens* – when we learned to domesticate seeds, plant them, monitor their growth, harvest them. This ancestral knowledge was passed from generation to generation and is the result of the agricultural revolution of the Neolithic period at the end of the Stone Age. When seeds are patented and genetically modified, the essence of humanity – sovereignty over the production of food – is threatened. With genetically modified crops, free seeds disappear and seeds with an owner emerge. Seeds created in a laboratory, controlled at the level of their DNA, able to grow but not to reproduce. If nothing is done, in a few decades perhaps all food production will be dependent on genetically modified crops, and autonomy in food production will be wiped out. All the knowledge garnered over more than ten thousand years of experience will end up imprisoned under patents controlled by fewer than ten global corporations and billions of people will be paying subsidies to very few; a new form of slavery; a new humanity, or one that will replace it. With information technology the same thing is happening: knowledge becomes immured in closed-source code and restricted by proprietary software. The essence of the Digital Culture programme for the *Ponto de Cultura* network is to inspire the *Pontos* (and the people) to pursue collaborative and generous ways of working; that is why we use open-source software.

To me, it was in Piauí that Brazil fully 'unhid' itself. Talking to the *Pontos de Cultura*, meeting people from diverse initiatives, various things fell into place. I saw young people exercising new forms of citizenship and social commitment. The *Ponto de Cultura* programme made a great difference in that state. I saw the impact of the programme on my travels around Brazil, but on that visit it was clearer. In twenty-four hours, I saw Brazil changing; and it was in Piauí.

Postscript: I also met with the state governor, Wellington Dias. He had personally negotiated the *Ponto de Cultura* network for the state. Initially, 30 were planned, then he requested it be enlarged to 60, offering to increase the matching funds. We accepted. Hours later, he called requesting 20 more, as he wanted to reach 50 state municipalities (added to the 30 already active, the state would have a total of 110 *Pontos*) and set a target for 2010 of 100 per cent of municipalities with at least one *Ponto de Cultura*. It was impossible to deny such a request. It is more common for governors not even to remember culture in their plans. I wanted to thank and congratulate him for his efforts. It was a rapid meeting, as Piauí was under a state of emergency due to heavy rains, but even so there was time for us to talk about the importance of culture as a factor for development: in Piauí, in Brazil and in the world.

7. PONTO DE CULTURA
The construction of a public policy

Straight to the (cultural) point – A new kind of state, listening to voices that have never been heard

Participatory and transformative, the policy that brought about the *Pontos de Cultura* aims to set new parameters for administration and democracy in the relationship between state and society. Instead of imposing a programme of culture, or inviting groups to tell us what culture they want or need, we ask *how* they want it. Instead of culture being understood as a product, it is recognised as a process. This new way of thinking was expressed in our 2004 legislation for the selection of the first *Pontos de Cultura*. We inverted the normal contract that the state establishes with whoever it is funding: the Ministry of Culture set out the budget it could offer and the recipients decided how to spend it, according to their own requirements and perspective.

Ponto de Cultura is in itself a concept of public policy. The *Pontos* are cultural organisations which gain strength and recognition when a partnership – a contract – is made with the state. There is a subtle distinction to be made here. The *Ponto de Cultura* is not for the people, but of the people: an organiser of culture at a local level, serving as both receiver and transmitter. The *Ponto de Cultura* operates not as a government agency or service provider but as a node in a network. Its focus is not on needs, or on a lack of social infrastructure and services, but on the potential of individuals and groups, and their capacity for agency. The *Ponto de Cultura* is culture as process, developing social autonomy and community protagonism.

The creation of a *Ponto de Cultura* begins when an agreement is signed between the group that runs it and the government so that they can define responsibilities (for example, the *Ponto* must give access to the public, work collaboratively, and share its decision-making with the community) and rights (financial processes, monitoring and train-ing, public access to assets and services purchased with the funding, etc.). Some are NGOs focused on social and educational action, others are *samba* schools, local community associations, indigenous villages, theatre groups, conservatoires, academic extensions of universities, museums, rural settlements or cooperatives. Each has its own characteristics and structure.

There is inevitable tension around the implementation and monitoring of *Pontos de Cultura*. On one side, there are the cultural groups competing to acquire public resources and infrastructure, on the other, the state with its norms of strict regulation and control. But the tension has an educational role that, in the long term, can achieve changes on both sides. Our goal is a state bureaucracy that is more flexible and better suited to the realities of life, as well as the creation of a social movement better equipped in dealing with management problems, capable of supporting public policy and planning its own activities.

This interaction, though initially difficult, creates an entirely new state model. In the conventional models, we must choose between burdensome forms of the state, characterised by intervention and bureaucracy, or the *laissez-faire* state, with little sensitivity to social needs. A 'new type' of state shares power with people, listens to those who have never been heard, talks with those who have never had a voice, and sees the invisible members of its population: utterly present, but with a touch as light as air.

> '*We, the people of Santo in Pernambuco, now have increased self-esteem.... candomblé has always been treated with intolerance. The police have looted us time after time, and stolen essential artefacts which are thrown like dirt into the basement of the Palácio do Campo das Princesas; ibas, the ilu, the assentamentos. Now, when the police show up, we say: "What do you want?" We are a Ponto de Cultura, recognised by the federal government....*'
> Beth de Oxum, *Ponto de Cultura Memória e Produção da Cultura Popular – Coco de Umbigada*, Olinda, Pernambuco

Does this process risk institutionalising the existing cultural movements, which will then lose their spontaneity or even become co-opted to a state agenda? Of course it does. Faced with this risk, a political culture of liberation is essential. By 'institutionalisation' we mean the contamination of a 'lifeworld' (culture, society, people) by 'systems' (state, market). To resist this we need to help develop and strengthen the skills of groups and individuals, their connections to each other and their ability to act as historical agents. Thus we can open new channels for mutual understanding and affirmation of identities, both social and personal.

The *Ponto de Cultura* can be (or at least wants to be) a place to reject the increasing fragmentation of modern life, building a collective identity from diversity and forging interconnections between different cultural practices. The formula which supports the theory of the

Pontos de Cultura was arrived at through empirical observation of real case studies. It can be expressed as a simple equation, where Autonomy + Protagonism result in an environment favourable to the breaking down of relationships of dependency or welfare, which so frequently result from government policies.

This new framework represents a breakthrough in public policy and will realise its potential if the process results in more nodes on the network. The more nodes and networks there are, the more sustainable the empowerment process initiated by the *Ponto de Cultura* will be. This equation acknowledges that a *Ponto de Cultura* is only fully achieved when it is connected in a network.

The network of *Casas de Cultura* in Campinas – evolution of the concept

Marquesa. A maid whose first name bears the weight of a title from nobility. And her intentions were noble. A resident of a peripheral suburb of Campinas in São Paulo state – Parque Itajaí – she gathered a group of mothers and went to the public library with this proposal: 'We want training to help us guide our children when they are using books. And we want books, too, because the nearest library is twenty kilometres away from our homes.'

TC. The nickname of Antonio Carlos Santos da Silva, just one more Silva among millions in Brazil. In the 1970s, he attended a supplementary high school and popular theatre course at Evolução de Campinas College. Musician and militant in the black consciousness movement, he didn't wait for help from anyone. He composed songs, made silk-screen posters, travelled (and travels) to peripheral and rural areas of Brazil, weaving a network of huts and planting baobab seedlings – the African tree of memory, which in the time of slavery became a tree of forgetfulness.

At the same time that Marquesa went to the library (1990), TC sought support to convert an old Cobal [Brazilian Food Company] warehouse into a *Casa de Cultura* in a poor neighbourhood of Campinas, Vila Castelo Branco. Thus began the network of 13 *Casas de Cultura* in the city. Designed as community spaces, each house received a small library with 500 books, training guidelines for reading, a community agent (recruited from the community and receiving a monthly minimum wage), art workshops, free tickets to shows made in two local theatres and support for local events or social 'nodes', such as holiday clubs for children. A simple action, nothing grand, grounded in realism and in the generosity of our people. As the Brazilian geographer Milton Santos said, 'The solution to Brazil's problems will come from scarcity ... and from the grass roots.' Most of the *Casas de Cultura* were created in converted buildings, sometimes a community centre or a show home in a new housing estate. The *Casa* acted as a central point, connecting with other local resources, such as a school-yard, a community auditorium or church hall. A broad programme of services at a low unit cost, which took advantage of and shared the community's existing infrastructure.

I was Municipal Secretary of Culture at the time (1990–2). At first, I thought that the process was irreversible and the life expectancy of *Casas de Cultura* would not be impaired by changes in municipal administration. My belief was not well-founded. The change of government brought delays in paying community workers' salaries, a loss of confidence in local initiatives and the break-up of the *Casas'* Board of Managers. This deterioration led to a loss of protagonism, and, over time, courses and workshops were cut and cultural program-ming became irregular and disconnected from local aspirations. The cultural community agents lost heart and the *Casas de Cultura* stopped producing regularly, losing audiences and connections. Losing life. Amongst these casualties was the show home that the people of Itajaí had transformed into a *Casa de Cultura*, the noble space created by Marquesa.

How the *Tainã Casa de Cultura* survived funding shortages and government bureaucracy

Tainã, a bird. That was the name of the *Casa de Cultura* founded by TC. Since he was accustomed to scarcity, he and his people carried on, regardless of the lack of support from the Municipality of Campinas. The *Casa* remained open with vibrant programming, drumming work-shops, screen printing, musical composition, a library, a kitchen, a community oven (communal eating being a form of culture), and later a media centre and steel drum orchestra, with amazing melody. In 2005, the *Tainã* became a *Ponto de Cultura* recognised by the federal government and, in 2006, President Lula personally conferred on it the Order of Cultural Merit.

Of course, the managers of the other houses were also used to coping with scarcity and are also brave, fighting people. So what made *Tainã* tougher, to survive and go further than the others? Autonomy.

Autonomy comes not through simply transferring responsibilities from the state to a *Ponto*. Autonomy preserves the ability to take and implement decisions with available resources. Autonomy is built through experience and networking. It is acquired in the search for knowledge, through relationships with peers and interactions with the authorities, be they masters of the oral traditions or large institutions. Autonomy is a practice: specific actions of participation and social affirmation. Autonomy is an exercise in freedom.

The *Tainã Ponto de Cultura* in Campinas, like the bird it was named after, gained wings and flew. Their free flight was possible because of their autonomy. But how did they achieve it?

Before the *Tainã* bird took flight, the protagonism of those who went on to set up the *Ponto de Cultura* had already been established. The protagonism of a social movement is apparent in the way that its members and their organisations understand each other as being the ones in control of their particular practice. These are individuals who make interventions in reality, from day-to-day activity to the writing of local development strategies. Cultural policy makers, whether (neo)liberal ('culture is good business') or Enlightenment ('bringing light to the uneducated masses') take away society's most precious qualities: its autonomy and its protagonism. If culture is thought of only as a product, synonymous with development or commerce, the people will be kept offstage.

When the state's policies do not recognise the cultural creations of the *paneleiras* (potters) of Goiabeiras in Vitória in Espírito Santo, or the toy master in the Vale do Jequitinhonha, they deprive them of their protagonism, treat them as folklore, primitive cultural expression or 'naïve' art. This destroys what should be an equal relationship between society and the administration in power. This failure of recognition is rooted in the idea that 'culture' is linked to 'civilisation'. Culture is then thought of as the means of measuring the development, progress, modernisation and refinement of the nation. The 'naïve' must be placed in its 'proper place': a museum piece, an innocent piece of craft work, a formless mass to be shaped. And the system remains dominant.

These concepts give birth to 'interventionist' management models of cultural administration. As guidelines are created that give recognition and validity to some cultural events, and not to others, society's cultural heritage becomes incomplete, taking away from the vast majority of people the full exercise of their citizenship (or their stage). Denying protagonism to this majority and presenting the elite – any elite – as the sole proprietor of knowledge and good taste is an efficient way of ensuring that dominance endures and the class system is legitimised. The 'other', the 'naïve', is offered like a pasteurised culture, manufactured to meet the average needs and tastes of a public that need not question what it consumes.

Protagonism and the networked structure are essential to the process of constructing the autonomy of *Pontos de Cultura*. This was why *Tainã* survived, and flocked to other *Pontos*, or birds, which cried as they flew: 'Here culture is made.'

Empowering ruins: when freedom of experiment and the protagonism of the young make a difference

At the end of the twentieth century, a musician called Alemberg returned home to his native town of Nova Olinda in Ceará. His objective: *Casa Grande*, a family heirloom that was in ruins. Legend has it that it was a haunted house. He decided to rebuild it, and received help from young people, children, women and the elderly, since most of the adult men had left town to seek employment in other places.

Once the house was rebuilt, they began to set up an archaeological museum. Vale do Araripe is not only the site of many fossils but is also rich in cave paintings. Prehistoric life was connected to the contemporary lives of the local community, who were training in conservation. Someone had the idea of letting local children write the captions for the exhibition, so everyone could understand them. And that is what they did.

It was a very large house and had room for many more activities. But the needs were even larger than the building.

Young people wanted to produce music, they created a band: not one, several. There was no cinema, so they set up a video library. Books were in short supply, so a library was created. They lacked a theatre: a theatre was built. All very modest and using only the resources available, but done with great care and everything that a good cultural centre needs: a stage with scenery and lights, a sound desk and good quality amplifiers, an auditorium with raked seating, a place for reflection, a foyer. Benefiting from a local museum, theatre, bands, quality films and books that would rarely have been seen in the valley, the residents wanted yet more: a radio station, internet, a local TV station.

Those tuning their radios into *Casa Grande* may be surprised to find high quality music programming: African music, traditional cowboy chants, jazz, interviews, Popular Brazilian Music … All researched, produced and introduced by children and young people. Tourists who stay a few days in the area to visit the waterfalls and caves with their rock inscriptions, or go horseback riding on cattle trails at night, can watch an Italian neo-realist movie, the new Danish Dogme film or a film from Brazil's Northeast. All they need to do is to borrow a movie from the *Casa Grande*'s video library. Or watch a local TV programme, also designed, produced, directed and managed by young people and children. At first the station broadcast on an open frequency, but it was closed for not having a licence: it was claimed that the signal would disturb the air traffic which, to this day, the boys try to catch a glimpse of in the skies over the valley of the flying dinosaurs. After the banning of the open broadcasts, the TV station got a new name: *Sem Canal* (Without Channel), alluding to a famous newsreel of the 1960s and 70s called the *Canal Cem* (Channel 100). Each week a new film will be showing in the theatre of the *Ponto de Cultura*. Adults sit in the audience and only appear as interviewees, since the plot, script, direction and acting are all created by the children and young people.

There is also a band for the very young where the children play toys, instruments of their own invention, creating sound with their mouths or by drumming on tin cans, pots and plastic buckets. Slightly older children form their own bands, with real musical instruments (of course the toys and buckets are real musical instruments too!). The young people who played in the first toy band are now around twenty years of age and have gone on to set up an experimental jazz band, mixing rock with rapping, Popular Brazilian Music, and popular styles from the Northeast, *xote* and *baião*. As a *Ponto de Cultura* they performed in Germany at Popkomm (The Music Media Campus) in 2006. Some of them are now leaving their home town – not migrating to look for work any more, but seeking out higher education, studying music, theatre, anthropology, architecture, film and engineering. Their heads are conquering the world, but their feet are firmly planted in Araripe.

This is radical empowerment, which can only exist when it grows out of autonomy, sown by initiative. Alemberg and his wife, Rosane, an archaeologist, no longer live in the city (although they are always around) and the *Ponto de Cultura* of *Casa Grande* is growing stronger. The *Ponto*'s managers are the children and young people; one coordinates its publishing, another is the playground manager, coordinator of radio or TV programming, another runs the participatory budgeting of *Casa Grande* (published as a public document, detailing everything from the smallest item of income – the sale of a piece of cake – to the simplest of the expenses). Each activity is someone's responsibility, and they rotate these positions among themselves. Young people who grew up in the *Casa Grande* learned from hands-on experience and decided to stay in its valley, breaking the cycle of exodus that took everyone away.

Over time, the news travelled the world and visitors began to come, a different kind of tourism, the type that wants to change its own way of seeing by communing with the locality. Three thousand visitors a month, in search of the waterfalls and rock paintings, listening to chants, the culture of the semi-arid *sertão* and the amazing initiative of the youngsters from *Casa Grande*.

With the *Ponto*, a new economy was created in Nova Olinda, democratic and sustainable. It became necessary to host the tourists, so family hostels were created; a simple, comfortable suite in the backyard of the parents (especially mothers) of boys and girls of the *Ponto de Cultura*. Leather crafts were reinvigorated, with the master craftsman Expedito and many other masters and apprentices who now find a market for their purses, shoes and theatrical props. Sustainable cultural tourism generates new sources of income for the community's families. And the adults begin to return to the city. More income in the city, and well distributed, because it is shared among many people.

Casa Grande with its reputation as a haunted house, enabled residents to appreciate themselves and their city more, finding their own place in the world, whose centre had always existed.

Emancipatory culture

Autonomy, ownership and empowerment are the pillars of the democratic and transformative infrastructure of the *Pontos de Cultura*; principles that are derived from my observation of real-life situations, and also, in a way, from my frustration with seeing the deactivation of the *Casas de Cultura* in Campinas. I was very young when I was Municipal Secretary of Culture, and I needed to understand this short period in my life and learn from its mistakes. Luckily, I had the opportunity to reapply the method and concept on a national scale at the Federal Ministry of Culture.

What was the real basis for the success of the cultural centres in Campinas? If they were so necessary, and spread so quickly, why did they fade away so easily? What was missing? What made the *Tainã*'s destiny different? Why is the experience of *Casa Grande* so striking?

The *Casas de Cultura* arose from practical needs, a group of mothers wanting to provide cultural activities for their children, artists in search of training, communities trying to improve their environment. But were they built on stable foundations? Perhaps the programme was implemented more as a result of my desire and the will of individual groups, and there was confusion between the legitimate demand of small groups and the aspirations of a whole community. It certainly needed more time to mature: the programme lasted less than two years. After this experience, during those moments when bureaucracy and power struggles seem to dominate, I take a deep breath and repeat the mantra: 'give it time, give it time …'; and never give up.

What set *Tainã* apart from Parque Itajaí was that it was rooted more deeply in the community, whereas Itajaí's *Casa de Cultura* was founded as the neighbourhood itself was being formed, when neighbours barely knew each other. What is significant in the experience of *Casa Grande* is a continual search for experimentation, shared responsibilities, the purity with which they found solutions without fear of ridicule or making mistakes, the confidence they had in themselves whilst still holding on to their curiosity and interest in learning from each other.

To focus on only one of the concepts would be a mistake. Autonomy and protagonism are complementary when they form a triad with empowerment. They make up the stable tripod of cultural sustainability in communities. These three foundations cannot be understood statically but rather as building blocks of values, their importance increasing when they multiply each other. These are values that generate a new concept: the *Ponto de Cultura*.

This is a different route to inclusion and social sustainability, and involves not only training in specific skills for the particular cultural role of each group, but also a process of social, digital, cultural, economic and political inclusion. The realisation of these notions and concepts gives rise to a new political culture characterised by freedom, where the *Ponto de Cultura* breaks down social and political hierarchies and lays the foundations for the building of a new legitimacy.

The interconnectedness of individuals

Scholars and experts usually divide social movements into two distinct categories. 'Traditional' social movements include trade unions, community associations, and student organisations; movements that tend to be structured hierarchically. This model of social organisation has suffered serious erosion since the end of the twentieth century and has found great difficulty in responding to the demands of the very sectors that it purports to represent.

'New' social movements form another model. Examples can be found in hip hop, environmentalism, cooperatives and community radio stations, or movements built around personal identity, such as the women's movement, civil rights or gay rights movements. There are also NGOs focused around an issue, a geographical area or a social group. Although they are included in the same category, these two types of movement have very different social backgrounds. One aims to forge connections and solidarity among peripheral communities and those excluded from property and rights; the other is born from the middle class, and seeks to make connections through an identity based on allegiance to a cause. Although they need to be viewed as different movements, bringing together very different social subjects, these non-governmental organisations have become an important example of the creation of new relationships between state and society.

Yet another category of social organisations are those linked to traditional communities and non-political initiatives, which can be defined as cultural groups: *quilombola* communities descended from escaped slaves, indigenous communities, those working with traditional rhythms and popular dances like *samba* schools, *maracatu* [which maintains the cultural traditions of slaves from the sugar plantations in the Northeast], *cirandas* [the circle dances of the women of Northeastern fishing communities], *quadrilhas* [the square dances which travelled from Regency ballrooms in Europe to local communities across Brazil], *capoeira* and other activities of a cultural/religious nature. The 'exclusion' of these groups immunised their organisations against the dilemmas affecting 'traditional' social movements (political or representative) and 'new' social movements (of thematic or fragmented character), preserving their fluidity and agility. But it also segregated them, separating them from the broader movement for social change.

Cut off from dialogue with a changing world, many of these movements lost their vitality and became hidden and self-absorbed, or were taken over by the market or by politics, as in the case of *samba* schools in the big cities. Easily classified as 'folklore', they remain inaccessible and incomprehensible to other sections of society. But they are extremely light and uncomplicated in their organisational forms, and they exist with a creative tension between tradition and invention.

These movements were creating underground forms of political rights long before ideas of civil society or modern concepts of citizenship had established themselves among us. They took to the

streets and sugarcane plantations during festivals, affirming their identities and exercising solidarity. Those who follow a *Folia de Reis* [a
musical procession celebrating the journey of the Three Kings, part of
traditional Catholic/*candomblé* nativity festivities] can see that it is a
product of collectivism. Someone donates props or fabrics, others sew
clothes; at each house on the journey there is a plate of food, sometimes placed on the windowsill to be surreptitiously stolen as part of
the game. Thus the participants of the *Folia de Reis* survive for days
on end, and popular culture survives for centuries.

Often excluded from public policy, traditional modes of cultural
expression are asserting themselves through the *Ponto de Cultura*
programme as unique agents in the political sphere. The *Cultura Viva*
programme brings together these various movements, classified here
into three types:

i)   those defined by allegiance to a cause;
ii) new social movements;
iii) cultural and traditional expression.

The interconnectedness of social individuals and their development
with autonomy, protagonism and empowerment are complementary.
The *Cultura Viva* programme's agenda of stimuli can generate a new
form of public policy and political culture. Unlike the old structures
that are laid down in management textbooks or guidance for public
administration, *Cultura Viva* has no guidelines to follow as it stimulates
and strengthens pre-existing social and cultural energies. It validates
social experience.

A democratic and transformative infrastructure is realised in this
process of state and society coming together and sharing responsibilities, in which public officials and social movements establish
dialogue and channels for mutual learning. We have taken a path
that rethinks the state, that widens its definitions and functions by
opening its doors to share power and knowledge with both the
traditional and unrepresented people in society, sharing space and
seeking new opportunities.

Tuning the concept

The term *Ponto de Cultura* was introduced in the late 1980s, when the
anthropologist Antonio Augusto Arantes was Secretary of Culture in
the city of Campinas and I worked with him as head of the Museums
Division. The first space to bear the name was the *Ponto de Cultura*
in Joaquim Egídio, a mountainous rural district of old coffee farms and
derelict great houses.

The fundamental difference between the *Ponto de Cultura* and the *Casa de Cultura* is that, even when it is shared with the community, the *Casa* is purpose-built and the direct result of government action. The government builds or adapts the space, decides the location and sets the schedule. In the *Critical Dictionary of Cultural Policy*, Professor Teixeira Coelho notes that these spaces imply a 'territorial removal of culture or cultural practices: practices belonging to a particular place are transposed to another, with which they have no historical or social connection. This artificiality of origin is so evident and accentuated that it is often identifiable as the main reason for the decay or under-utilisation of the centre's resources and potential.' With the *Pontos de Cultura*, the process is reversed; the government's job is to recognise and enhance the community's own cultural initiatives, in the place where they occur. Cultural activity and place are intrinsically linked.

Another recurring question is whether the *Ponto de Cultura* replaces the need for other cultural facilities. Rather the opposite: the *Ponto de Cultura* creates favourable conditions for the consolidation of grassroots culture, providing the most durable means of achieving the best libraries, well-equipped theatres, dynamic cultural centres, vigorous museums and policies that support training, production and the transmission of cultural activity.

The dimensions of culture

Understanding culture as a process presupposes that we perceive the way various dimensions of life are woven together. Under the direction of Gilberto Gil as Minister of Culture, the Ministry adopted a wider, anthropological definition of culture; culture as the production of symbols, citizenship and economy. The *Cultura Viva* programme and the *Ponto de Cultura* initiated that concept, but as the programme developed I realised it was necessary to go further.

Art cannot be restricted to the symbolic arena. In addition to the production of symbols, art involves skill, all the skills of humanity (from the Latin root *artem*, skill) and understanding of meaning through sensory perception. The *Ponto de Cultura* involves the demolition of traditional cultural narratives, monopolised by a few, and a sensitive and strategic partnership to achieve a narrative shift which reveals that the 'invisible' can be seen and have a voice. This – not the metaphysical defence of 'universal beauty' or 'art for art's sake' – is the true realisation of the aesthetic movement. Art reflects the aspirations and contradictions of its historical context and is simultaneously the product and the vector of social change. So that beyond the preoccupation with pure beauty, we try everything in our power to allow cultural affirmation of the subjectivity of individuals, groups and social classes. And that quest must be undertaken with charm, beauty and high quality, for without these, barriers will not break down and stereotypes will endure.

The same thing happens in the civic dimension. It is essential that we achieve full rights and participation in cultural dialogue, but it would be reductive to limit the *Ponto de Cultura* to the scope of citizenship or of popular culture. Cheap sound bites about 'cultural inclusion' or 'social inclusion through culture' are even worse. The *Ponto de Cultura* works with popular culture and social inclusion and has a clear role in citizenship, but it is primarily a cultural programme: culture as a means of interpreting the world and an expression of values and feelings, culture as a means of mutual understanding and collaboration. In this sense it would be more appropriate to classify the *Ponto de Cultura*'s operation as falling within the field of ethics.

We must deepen our concept of economy, too. What type of economy do we want? A government survey showing that 8 per cent of Brazil's GDP comes from culture demonstrates the economic reality of cultural activities (IBGE – Brazilian Institute of Geography and Statistics). But in what context should we locate the so-called 'creative economy'? Capitalism appropriates every ounce of goods and riches produced on the face of the earth (and below the surface, and in the future, perhaps, far beyond the planet) and transforms both tangible and intangible assets into mere commodities. The *Ponto de Cultura* does not aim to place culture within these commercial processes or to alienate it from real life.

The new understanding built by this process is that if the economy can determine a culture, then culture can also determine the economy. By adopting a new cultural attitude we can change economic relationships, paving the way for an economy of solidarity, based on consumer awareness, fair trade and collaborative work. I can see the sparks of new economic relations, especially in the *Teia* [annual national meeting of *Pontos de Cultura*, literally a spider's web or network], as it connects the *Pontos de Cultura* with Centres of Economic Development, supported by the Ministry of Labour.

The *Ponto de Cultura* is integration within diversity. 'The part is in the whole, the whole is in the part'; quantum physics proves this ancient wisdom, which has been abandoned with the fragmentation of modern life. After five years of implementing the *Ponto de Cultura* programme, I understand that the rapprochement between aesthetics, ethics and economics is essential for the structuring of human life and

can cement a new meaning for culture and for civil society. They cannot be separated, the 3 'Es' of culture:
Ethics
Æsthetics
Economics.

The *Ponto de Cultura* becomes public policy

Twelve years passed between the experience in Campinas and my invitation to take up the post of Secretary of Cultural Programmes and Projects at the Ministry of Culture. My appointment was made directly by the incoming Executive Secretary at the Ministry, Juca Ferreira, and so rapidly that I was appointed before the Minister of Culture, Gilberto Gil, had even met me. I was soon presented with the planned programme: constructing prefab cultural facilities in the suburbs and outskirts of large cities and slums – BACs: Bases for Cultural Support. But there was a big problem: I completely disagreed with the proposal.

There was no concept, only a prefab architectural project. Hollow structures, to be given to the community to look after. Standardised buildings in such a diverse country? Who would run them, pay the bills? And the programme? Everything run on a voluntary basis? It would never work.

I needed to act fast. I had to offer a new proposal to replace the BACs. I completely disagreed with the primacy given to these buildings, but the programme had its supporters and the main enthusiast was President Lula himself. As I would be responsible for rolling out the BACs, it would be best to make my position clear and, if necessary, I would not take up the post, rather than wasting time (my own and the government's). Before my appointment was published in the Official Gazette we had written a new programme. *Cultura Viva* was the name we chose, because culture is alive and constantly renewing. I discussed the idea with Augusto Arantes, president of the Institute of Historic and Artistic Heritage, and everything became clear: we would adopt the name *Ponto de Cultura* to express this new concept.

I remember a comment by Márcio Meira, then Secretary of Institutional Cooperation at the Ministry of Culture: 'The *Ponto de Cultura* is to national culture what family doctors and local clinics are to the unified Public Health System.'

The decision to re-use the term *Ponto de Cultura* also took its inspiration from Gilberto Gil. In his inaugural speech as Minister of Culture, Gil used the expression 'anthropological acupoints' to represent his intentions at the Ministry. Acupuncture is to massage vital points of the human body: unlock it, release energy. Acupoints go straight to the point. There was no doubt about the name.

When at last I was introduced to the Minister, he had already read the proposal and fully supported it. We talked about creative processes, cultural expressions, legitimacy, symbols, heartbeats, development through exchange. At the end he said: 'How interesting, instead of focusing on the structure you looked at the flow. And the flow is life.' A few days later, we announced the selection process for the first *Pontos de Cultura*.

Maracatu Rural in
Pernambuco. TTC

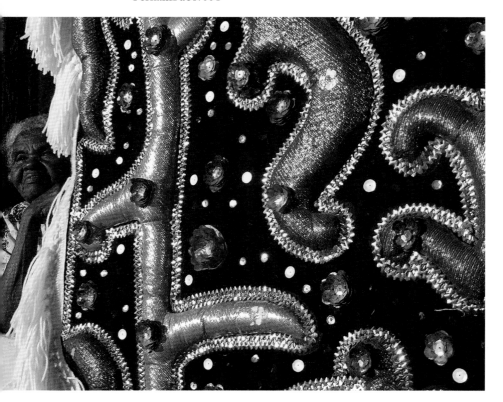

Participant in the closing event
of the 2008 *Teia*, Brasília –
'The Re-proclamation of the
Republic through Culture'. TTC

The closing procession
of the 2008 *Teia* passes
Brasília Cathedral on its
way from the bus station
to the presidential
palace. TTC

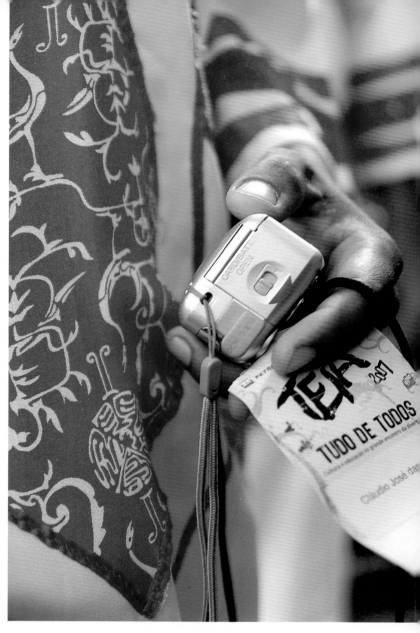

A participant arrives at the
2007 *Teia* in Belo Horizonte. RD

The network of 'oral culture' *Pontos* throughout Brazil is mapped in 2007. RD

Street theatre by a *Ponto de Cultura* from Rio Branco during the 2007 *Teia*. RD

Fashion show by
Rio-based *Ação
Comunitária do
Brasil* at the 2007
Teia. RD

88

Two young drummers
from *AfroReggae* in
Vigário Geral, a *favela* in
Rio de Janeiro. RD

Baba Israel, former Artistic
Director of Contact
Theatre in Manchester,
raps with a member of
AfroReggae during a
Points of Contact visit,
March 2010. RD

Madani Younis, former
Artistic Director of
Freedom Studios in
Bradford, during a *Points
of Contact* visit to Brazil
in 2010. RD

A young dancer from the
Rio *Ponto de Cultura
Grupo Nós do Morro* (We
from the Hillside) performs
for the British delegation
during a *Points of Contact*
visit, 2010. RD

Young students at
Spectaculu, Rio de
Janeiro, during a
workshop with
People's Palace Projects
Associate Artist Gary
Stewart in 2010. RD

An outdoor film screening
in the small town of Barra
do Mendes as part of a
national audiovisual
training project, *Revelando
os Brasis* (Revealing
Brazils), led by Instituto
Marlin Azul. RD

A screening in Carnaúba
dos Dantas as part of
Revelando os Brasis. RD

Banda Cabaçal do Crato,
from the *sertão do Cariri*,
performs at a meeting of
Northeastern *Pontos*. TTC

Interactive installation
created by young
students from *Spectaculu*,
Rio de Janeiro. RD

8. JONGO DA SERRINHA

Far away.

A state school. Drumming, clapping, circle dancing.

'I learned to dance with my Aunt Maria.'

'I've known the *jongo* since I was seven years old....'

Young people all talking at once, girls and boys singing and dancing to the music of the *quilombos*. 'My mother arrived at the Serrinha in 1910 and brought the *jongo* from Minas Gerais. I was born with the *jongo*, inside the womb,' says Aunt Maria, the owner of the courtyard where it all started; or restarted.

The courtyard begins to get crowded.

'The children themselves made us grow. We grew so much that we founded the *Centro Cultural*, after the *Ponto de Cultura*. It was the involvement of the children that inspired us to look for a greater focus on culture and education.' Two young women – Lazyr Sinval and Suelen Costa – coordinate the *Ponto de Cultura*, and recount its history for me, completing each other's sentences.

The *Ponto de Cultura Jongo da Serrinha* is part of its community through traditional culture. And it recreates itself.

They dance, tap their feet, clap their hands.

'Ta ta; ta ta, ta ta....'

'Here the children arrive and dance. Afterwards, there are singing lessons, *capoeira*, percussion, literature, theatre....'

'I was sleeping when the conga drum called me,
get up dear, captivity is over.
I was sleeping when the conga drum called me,
get up dear, captivity is over.'

The abolition of slavery in Brazil was not accompanied by agrarian reform and land rights, so the 'liberated' slaves went to the cities. Arriving in Rio de Janeiro, they went to live on the hilltops: Salgueiro, Mangueira, Serrinha ...

They stayed in Serrinha.

'Mountain of my golden dreams,
where we were raised....'

Originally, children were not participants in the *jongo* – until they themselves started to join in. 'They play the *jongo* rhythms on the refrigerator, on the cooker, at school. They are the ones who pass it on to their friends.' There are four dance steps: *amansa café, sabiando, contratempo* and *mancado*, the latter danced as if the person were limping, with one hand behind their back. 'And today the future of *jongo* is guaranteed by young people', Aunt Maria recognises.

'*Jongo* is a dance that belongs to the imprisoned slaves. We respect that.'

Sacred culture. With a *Ponto de Cultura*, a whole community rediscovers itself.

9. THE CULTURA VIVA PROGRAMME

A *Ponto de Cultura* presupposes socio-cultural autonomy and leader-ship, its potency realised through connectivity within a network; and it expresses itself in the recognition and legitimisation of the process of culture-making within communities, thus engendering social em-powerment. In itself, this public policy would already represent an advance on traditional forms of the relationship between public authority and society. But it is necessary to go further to bring about transformation. Thus the *Cultura Viva* programme.

The aim of the programme is to integrate the *Ponto* within a wider system: alive, pulsating. If the *Ponto de Cultura* is the point (base) of support, *Cultura Viva* is the lever. Just as the heart and lungs beat in rhythm together to ensure a continuous flow of life, the *Ponto de Cultura* works to unite initiatives and *ações* ('actions', or formal programmes). It is these 'actions' that guarantee the vitality of the system, constantly feeding it with new questions, ideas and initiatives, spinning together a web composed of infinite points that used to be isolated, but now see themselves as components of something greater. The programme is always unfinished. 'Where there is life, there is incompleteness,' as the Brazilian educational reformer Paulo Freire used to say.

If *Ponto de Cultura* is simplicity, *Cultura Viva* is complexity; each completes the other. It is the 'actions' and interactions of *Cultura Viva* that ensure it maintains its characteristic subversiveness: between the state and society; within the internal apparatus of the state; in creating alliances with NGOs and social movements (which themselves undergo internal changes when they participate in the *Ponto de Cultura* network); and, above all, in the process of creative questioning of culture itself.

Much more than the construction of buildings or the simple transfer of resources to cultural organisations, the programme's aim is to intensify the interaction between individual subjects and their environment, promoting development from the sharing of ideas and values, enabling people to take part in the world they experience. The programme brings with it strong components of enchantment and magic, power and affection. In his inaugural speech as Minister of Culture in January 2003, Gilberto Gil expressed this desire from the outset: '... to clear paths, open clearings, stimulate, shelter. Perform a kind of anthropological acupuncture, massaging meridians and spaces which have become temporarily unvalued or dormant in the cultural body of the nation.... It will be the space for trying new directions; the space of opening up to popular creativity and new languages; the space for adventure and risk; and the space for memory and invention.' *Cultura Viva* gave this desire form and content.

When I travelled around Brazil and held meetings with *Pontos de Cultura*, I realised that this sharing is real. The programme has faced numerous difficulties; bureaucracy, unrealistic rules, delays in the payment of grants to young people, late payments to the *Pontos*, an accounting process bogged down and unfit for the real world. The actual resources that are distributed to each *Ponto* are not so significant: R$60,000 (£20,000) per year in 2008, the equivalent to R$5,000 (£1,333) per month. Despite its limitations, the programme has been enthusiastically received and supported. Participants have taken *Cultura Viva* for themselves; they have appropriated the values of the programme and have started to identify themselves as a social movement, even defining themselves as '*ponteiros*'.

A new form of militancy is emerging with an effective social basis. Research conducted by IPEA (Instituto de Política Econômica Aplicada – the government's Institute of Applied Economic Research) involving 380 *Pontos de Cultura* showed that each *Ponto* reached an average of 3,300 people. With 2,500 *Pontos de Cultura* at the end of 2009, IPEA's calculations indicated that the programme was headed by 27,500 leaders, had inspired 750,000 activists and reached 8.25 million people. In addition to the members of the public who benefit from direct involvement in the cultural activities, there are indirect benefits, through improvements in the quality of life and the foundation of healthier social environments with greater sense of community.

When I wrote the conceptual framework of the programme, I deliberately replaced the term 'historical subject' with 'empowerment'. As a historian, I would be in a more comfortable position if I had used 'historical subject', as an expression more appropriate to the concept: the people adopting the role of 'agent'. But there was a risk in using the more precise concept that it was likely to bring on name-calling: '*Dirigistes*! Ideologues! Populists! Marxists!' and all the '-ists' that the ideological apparatus of the dominant classes use to abort new ideas. I calculated that 'empowerment' would face less resistance and would be easier to understand. I even joked to myself: 'the colonised minds will find it sophisticated and modern. Empowerment.'

Empowerment, however, presupposes a limited transfer of power to communities to resolve their little difficulties, without questioning the system as a whole. This would be a problem. The solution was to associate empowerment with the concepts of autonomy and leadership, bringing a new meaning and giving a Brazilian touch to the word. And thus, in the anthropophagic, cannibalistic Brazilian tradition, 'empowerment' has gained new strength and meaning in the mouth of the people.

Autonomy, leadership, empowerment, management via networks, free knowledge, open-source software, digital culture, shared work, intellectual generosity, the *griot* tradition of travelling storytellers. These are concepts and practices that are present in the militancy of those who are running the *Pontos de Cultura* all over Brazil. They are the ideas and values that increasingly underpin *Cultura Viva*, and the constant introduction of new *ações* (actions) or formal programmes, within the overall programme, test and refine their validity. A *Ponto de Cultura* that involves itself little in the formal *ações* finds it more difficult to make a qualitative leap in its work. It may continue to be (relatively) effective in its local community, but if the *Ponto* continues as an isolated group, the role of the programme will have been, at best, that of a good 'conduit' of public money. *Ações* within *Cultura Viva* boost networks, instigate ideas, expose contradictions, and it is in this interaction that the programme becomes effective.

Just as the *Ponto de Cultura* is not a creation, but activates the power of pre-exisiting cultural initiatives, the same happens with *ações* (actions). Initially, four *ações* were launched: Digital Culture, the *Cultura Viva* Agent, *Escola Viva* (Living School) and *Griô*. As the network of *Pontos de Cultura* has developed, other *ações* have been incorporated and our role has been rapprochement through diversity.

Digital Culture

When I arrived in government, the Ministry of Culture had already begun a dialogue with the digital culture movement. Cláudio Prado, a young/old hippie, led a large number of hackers and social networks of open-source software. For Cláudio, the digital is a culture, not a technology, incorporating values and behaviours arising from the use of open-source code, with collaborative work and free knowledge: 'digital culture hastens humanity towards a new era, involving paradigm shifts, representing a rite of passage from the economic era to a cultural era.' With the digital, it would be possible to promote leaps in civilisation, allowing 'communities who had been circumscribed by a nineteenth-century reality to leap directly to the twenty-first century, without the need to pass through the twentieth century and everything it represented in terms of social and economic values,' he concluded.

We held our first meeting. It was on a Saturday, amid paintings, books and old furniture at Cláudio's apartment in Rua Augusta, in the centre of São Paulo. There were young people from various sectors: university students, artists, rappers, social activists; a thousand ideas. I went to introduce myself and listen to them. I talked about the *Ponto* and connectivity through the network. They talked about the strengthening of collaborative work communities, recycling of computers for new and unimagined creative, social and cultural uses and the human need for autonomy regarding machines. I related this to the quest of those who had been denied access to the means of production, for autonomy in their relations with those who control them. We talked about the possibilities offered by digital cameras, garage studios, whole editing suites hosted on just one computer, of sampling, of composition through montage, mixing.

I asked them to design a kit of this equipment, at a cost of no more than R$20,000 (£6,650) per unit and which would be easy to use and maintain. I wanted the cultural agents to be able to record themselves, so we had to make the kit simple and replicable.

From this meeting the 'multimedia studio' was born; a kit with a video camera, mixing desk, microphones and three computers acting as an open-source software editing suite. Each *Ponto de Cultura* empowering itself by recording and producing its culture, with free studios spread across the country; with cultural groups in the peripheries of big cities, in *quilombos*, indigenous villages and rural encampments. The means of production in the hands of the producers (any similarity with the philosophical thought of Marx is not entirely coincidental). Films and songs produced and distributed directly by those who produce the culture. All narrated in the first person, without intermediaries.

Cultura Viva Agent

In the first announcement about the *Cultura Viva* programme, the intention was already clear: 'Actual cultural change will only be effective if it involves a change in mentalities and attitudes. And changing attitudes requires much more than investments in work and facilities, it requires investment in people, in people from our communities.'

In 2003, the Ministry of Employment created a First Job programme, designed to subsidise young people's first employment. The government offered a monthly subsidy of R$1,500 for each new position open to young people without work experience. It was a failure. Companies wanted to hire young people, but not those targeted by the programme: the least educated, the homeless, young black or *mulato* people, the poor, young people whose appearance did not conform to their standard. The programme was a poor fit with corporate culture. And so we proposed a partnership, following the launch of *Cultura Viva* in 2004. The funds could be used to finance 'cultural agents' in the *Pontos de Cultura*, at a cost of only R$900 a month.

The *Cultura Viva* Agent programme was put into practice only once – it was soon cut. But the principles contained in the first *Cultura Viva* document are worth restating here:

> *'In many cases, professional qualification programmes, instead of liberating, only reinforce the process of social exclusion of the unemployed person, or the young person in search of their first job who is unlikely to find formal employment. People are seen as excluding themselves in as much as, subliminally, they are told: "work exists, but you cannot find it because you have no qualifications". Thus, after being offered a quick course, all responsibility for not being able to find work is placed on the individual, reinforcing his sense of impotence and failure. In contrast, community activity based on solidarity can be a great source of satisfaction, emancipation and income for the long-term unemployed and young people in search of their first job. The aim is to open the way for a process of transformation in which the receivers progressively become active formulators.'*

A simple idea that we were able to test. It was put into practice again by the Municipal Department of Sport and Leisure in São Paulo for 5,500 young people and for unemployed adults over forty, and subsequently for 11,000 young people in *Pontos de Cultura*, in partnership with the First Job programme. The unit cost was low: a monthly grant of R$250 represented an annual cost of R$3,000 per person [approximately £1,000 at the time]. Unfortunately, I have not yet managed to convince the managers of public policies of its significance. Who knows? One day …

Another attempt at a federal level was made in 2009. Juana Nunes, Coordinator of Network Mobilisation in the Secretariat for Cultural Citizenship at the Ministry of Culture, created two experimental funding programmes with the Secretariat's own resources: *Escola Viva* Agent (aimed at secondary school teachers and students) and *Cultura Viva* Agent (for youth leaders within *Pontos de Cultura*). It was small-scale: 720 grants in 90 state schools and 180 *Pontos de Cultura*, but it was a showcase to demonstrate that it is possible to follow a different path, combining income, education and emancipation.

Escola Viva

A *Ponto de Cultura* in every school. That is how it should be. But it is not. Schools are stuck in old learning patterns, are closed in upon themselves, and are simply repeating formulaic teaching, disconnected from life. Perhaps the problem is not exactly in schools, but in the education system itself, corroded by impenetrable and institutionalised ideas, bureaucracy and habit. Stuck between rules and vested interests, the administration of an education system which is called 'public' has emphatically failed in its aims. Or perhaps it has fulfilled them? It depends on your point of view.

Escola Viva is an initiative – an *ação* – of the *Cultura Viva* programme. A network connecting schools and their communities, with culture as the connector. The key idea involves knowledge and mastery of artistic languages, engendering capacity for autonomy, creation and tolerance: an ongoing education, which should occur everywhere, across all generations, at all times. This is not what happens within the current educational system, which creates 'disabled citizens', as Milton Santos recognised. The quest for *Escola Viva* presupposes that an emancipating libertarian education will emerge. It aspires to an education that respects, values and qualifies teachers (including decent salaries and continuous training), which incorporates all methods, is open to informal knowledge and respects the student's role as an agent in their own development.

Being the most ubiquitous public state facility (in many places, the only one), a school can be a privileged doorway to cultural goods and services. It has the potential to be a venue for community expressions (of any sort), empowering individuals and groups and propagating feelings and behaviours based on affection, mutual respect, solidarity and a culture of peace. It is clear that there is a gulf between the schools we have and the schools we would like. And this is where the integration between the *Ponto de Cultura* and the school comes in.

Within the *Escola Viva* network, there are 114 *Pontos de Cultura* and schools working together. At the Clóvis Borges Miguel State School, in Serra, Espírito Santo, the students run a *Rádio Instrumental Educativa* (Educational Radio Station) and, on the outskirts of the city of Rio de Janeiro, at the Vicente Januzzi State College, there are classes that combine philosophy with Brazilian popular music. This is how the teacher Vânia Correa Pinto paid tribute when the school won the

Cultura Viva award: 'We have begun to believe that art really can exist, even at school. We believe that art can live and persist amidst broken chairs, graffiti-strewn walls, cracked windows, stones, bricks and sand. It can emerge here clear, alive and real....'

Escola Viva: indigenous narrators on the Rio Negro river in the Amazon; the hip hop network in the Baixada Fluminense; *Maracatu Piaba de Ouro* in Pernambuco; the African roots of art, culture and education at *Humbiumbi* in Belo Horizonte (Minas Gerais). *Escola Viva* releases a new series of capabilities, such as in the 'Neighbourhood as School' centres in Nova Iguaçu (Rio de Janeiro) and Hortolândia (São Paulo), where the city itself became the site for formal education. A permanent school, open and full-time.

Griô

'To start the conversation
I ask for the blessing of the eldest
Who give me wisdom
To perform these verses.'
Cordel introducing the *Ação Griô*

This is an initiative that makes us reflect on the sacred dimension of life and the logic of economic convenience based on sharing that is preserved by the traditional Brazilian cultures. When *candomblé* sanctifies a waterfall or a natural spring it is preserving life. When a *reisado* procession survives because everyone in the community offers something, even if it is a plate of food for the walkers, it is practising sharing, cultivating behaviour essential for social cohesion. These expressions of traditional culture break with the cycle of alienation and vulgarisation of life, and serve as a basis for the construction of a society based on equity and solidarity.

In contemporary societies, we are experiencing a process of transformation of desire, time and the soul itself. Everything has become a commodity. This has the result of alienating populations from the possibility of achieving autonomy and emancipation. It promotes individualism and selfishness, the transformation of everything and everyone into merchandise, the reification of being. Within this scenario, urban violence, disrespect of working for others, unfettered exploitation, a lack of love for one's neighbour all emerge. Everything loses its meaning and only profit matters.

However, only worshipping tradition does not solve the problem. At the end of the day, as the Marxist historian Eric Hobsbawm demonstrated, all traditions were invented at a specific moment: they are historical constructs and incorporate prejudices and ideologies. The same is true of pragmatism. There is nothing more backward than allowing oneself to be guided by common sense; behind consolidated ideas there are historical constructs, and pragmatism becomes the enemy of profound transformation, accommodating something without questioning. It is at this time that the need arises for tradition to reinvent itself and memory becomes pivotal in reformulating and reinterpreting life. An invention that shuffles and breaks hierarchies and proposes the construction of new legitimacies, without cultures being imposed or standardised. Popular wisdom, which is different from common sense, takes on a new role and informal knowledge is perceived in all its sophistication and profundity.

The intergenerational and multisector dialogue proposed by the *Ponto de Cultura Grãos de Luz e Griô*, with the reinvention of the *Roda da Vida* (Wheel of Life), appeared as an *ação*. Without creating a fixed pedagogy, I could see that this initiative from the interior of the state of Bahia would be worth sharing and replicating. The experience of the *Grãos de Luz e Griô* is an *ação* that brings together biocentric education with Paulo Freire's methods and local cultural traditions.

With the *Ação Griô*, cultural, mystic workshops are held, walks, discussion circles. It is the appreciation of ancestral knowledge: common, shared knowledge from the *mestres* – the community elders – which comes from the bottom of our souls. This *ação* had not been planned but it was something that was lacking. Digital culture, youth, school, *Ponto de Cultura*. The ancestral element from the land itself – a firm floor on which to step:

> 'Griot teaching
> Comes from a Ponto de Cultura
> In Lençóis, in Bahia
> Wheel of Life mixes
> The Grãos de Luz e Griô
> Child old teacher
> The creator and the creature.'

That is what was lacking. I asked for more details about their practice, about the oral tradition. *Griô* is the Brazilian version of the French *griot,* also an invented word by students of Sub-Saharan Africa – Mali, Senegal – who went to study in France. These words seek to give a common meaning to traditions that have variously been named by genealogists, performers, musicians and storytellers. The *griôs* wander from village to village keeping this strand of their culture alive. They are cultures with oral traditions, but are no less complex and profound than written cultures. The African master Tierno Bokar Salif states clearly: 'Writing is one thing, wisdom another. Writing is a photograph of wisdom, but is not the wisdom itself.' I learned this with a *Ponto de Cultura* and with Márcio Caíres, the *Velho Griô* (Old Griot), and Lilian Pacheco, an educator.

Ação Griô has become a national initiative of the *Cultura Viva* programme, and through it we have funded more than a hundred of the most diverse experiences.

> *'Every Ponto de Cultura*
> *Has its pedagogy*
> *Together in a network*
> *Ação Griô recreates itself*
> *Cultura Viva Programme*
> *A Brazil that farms*
> *Harvesting wisdom.'*

Each project selected promotes the integration of traditional knowledge and school learning. The successful projects receive small grants (R$450 per month) for up to six people per *Ponto:* the elder, the *griôs* and an apprentice *griô*, who make the connection between the school and the elders through the process of oral education. In 2009, there were more than 600 *griôs* spread all over Brazil. They are not all descendants of Africans, as the idea is not to restrict the *ação* to a single ethnic group. There are indigenous *griôs*, descendants of Europeans, coastal inhabitants, Asians; all popular wisdom in one action. *Capoeira* masters, prayer ladies, Bahian women cooking *acarajé*, toymakers, midwives, witchdoctors, singers, artisans: *mestres* that safeguard our history from generation to generation. They deserve to have their role redefined, as living treasures. 'Each elder who dies is a library that burns down' (*Mestre* Hampáte Bâ). This is *Ação Griô*.

Pontinho de Cultura

> *'What is it, what is it?*
> *When you lose it*
> *You never find it again?'*
> *(Answer: time)*

The *Ponto de Cultura Bola de Meia*, in the Vale do Paraíba, in São Paulo, develops its programme through riddles, toy making, games and singing. It has become a *Pontão* (Big *Ponto* – cultural hub); and an action of *Cultura Viva*.

Jacqueline Baumgratz and Celso Pan have brought together musicians, poets, psychologists and educators to create a *Ponto de Cultura* in a two-storey house that is their own home. Downstairs are the cultural and educational facilities, including a very functional theatre and the administration office. In their backyard they receive the children, many children.

'Today I was walking around
and I discovered how things are
and everything I saw was not the same
the flowers are
different
the creatures are
different
and the people are
different

And what do we have in common?
It is the heart that beats like this
Tum tum; tum tum.'
Poem by Jacqueline Baumgratz

Children's culture, playfulness, games. We are *Ludens, Homo Ludens,* said the philosopher Johan Huizinga. To him, 'the essence of the playful spirit is to dare, run risks, bear uncertainty and tension'. The meaning of the *Pontinho de Cultura* (Children's Culture Point) *ação* is to rediscover this spirit, to re-establish intergenerational links and perceive children as producers of culture, where reality is imagination.

Another network: open and varied. There are many people doing many wonderful things for children, and with children, and children are also doing things for themselves. Dona Edna, in a fishing village on the edge of the city of Maceió, opened her house to receive children. Today she lives in one room and everything else is the *Ponto de Cultura,* or *Pontinho:* her *Poleiro dos Anjos* (Perch of the Angels).... The playful ambience of the Hospital Pequeno Príncipe in Curitiba, where children with cancer have only the hospital to play in and see the world from the window of their rooms.... Around the hinterland of Brazil, children continue to chase mythical *Sacis* – the one-legged mythical mischief-maker – and a network of 250 *Pontinhos* became established.

The *Pontinho* is the *locus,* be it a physical venue or a state of spirit, in which children's culture develops. It is not culture that adults pass on to children, but the culture of the childhood environment. The culture in which eight-year-old children teach six-year-olds, six-year-olds teach four-year-olds; the first step towards a group consciousness. If the childhood game represents the imitation of adults, its transmission is conducted by the children themselves. Do these games reinforce prejudices? Without doubt. Even so, it is better to 'let them do', ensuring a space of complete freedom, creating environments of common understanding and friendship. We let the children play and discover the world with their games. And we play with them. Full stop.

Culture and Health

The boy and the girl

'Once upon a time, there was a boy who really liked to smile.

One day, the doctor told him he could not smile anymore and gave him some medicine, and he became very sad.

He spent many days and nights without smiling, and he could not even dream, he just cried and had nightmares. Everything was sadness.

Until one day a girl took a picture of him and when he saw that sad face in the photo he became horrified and promised that from now on he was going to smile.

Every day that the girl looked at him and showed him the photo he remembered that he had to smile and he smiled so much at her that he began to feel happy.

And he got used to it and every time he thinks about her, even though he may be sad, he feels happy again. He likes the girl a lot.'

Gilmar, five years of age, story told in hospital

The *ação* 'Culture and Health' is the girl taking the photo and making the boy happy. It may be in a hospital, it may also be in a sacred space of *candomblé*. Dona Albertina, a *quilombola* of Campinho, is a natural pharmacist, a wise woman of her community. She knows that corn silk is used 'to lower blood pressure' and camomile works for 'stomach aches, intestinal cramps and inflammation of a baby's skin, as well as being a sedative and working against allergies'. Comfrey 'heals wounds', wormseed 'combats parasites in the intestines'. Dandelion 'is a good diuretic and recommended for when the woman's breast becomes engorged during breast-feeding'. Aniseed is 'for heartburn'. Macela 'aids digestion'; salvia 'for gingivitis and ulcers', guava 'for vaginal washing and tea for fevers and diarrhoea', and on the day of childbirth, cotton 'to avoid haemorrhaging, bathe the woman and increase the speed of the contractions'. Childbirth at home, humanised, *Cais do Parto*, a network of midwives.

The healing circles and circular dances, the *Meninas de Sinhá*, who one day decided to do something more than stay at home and complain about becoming old, so got together to sing songs from their childhoods and adolescence. And they laughed. And the pain began to go away.

A new network of 60 *Pontos*, from the Conceição Hospital Group and its 10 *Pontos de Cultura*, in Porto Alegre, to the art classes held by Olga Kos and her children with Down's syndrome. The drum of health of *Tainã* and the young people who guide adolescents in preventing sexually transmitted diseases. We set up the 'Culture and Health' network with an award of R$15,000 for *Pontos de Cultura* with a specific health proposal or focus. There was the prize-giving ceremony, a seminar, the exchange of experiences. This created a new network, a new *ação*. Now the *Pontos* get to know each other, they talk to each other. And they pass their experience on to others.

Free Media *Pontos*

Another network. Another initiative under the *Cultura Viva* programme: 'Culture and Communication' – *Pontos de Mídia Livre* (Free Media Points). While the *Ponto de Cultura* is a space for measuring the relationship between the state and society, it also exists in the relationship between groups and individuals. A mediator is a point of communication: if it is free, then it is Free Media.

In 2008, Brazil held its first Free Media meeting for media that are independent both of the state and of the market: from photocopied fanzines to blogs, websites, independent news agencies, magazines, community radio and TV channels – everything that allows free communication. One of the resolutions was to seek a public policy that could serve this social field, such as the *Ponto de Cultura*. We listened and we then created an *ação*. A few months later, in January 2009, a new funding programme was launched at the World Social Forum in Belém.

It is still a small gap, a crack that has started to open, as with the *Ponto de Cultura*. We began with R$4.7 million and planned 72 initiatives: *Pontos de Mídia* (R$40,000 for each one – approximately £13,500) and *Laboratórios de Mídia* (R$120,000 each), for national initiatives and for diffusion to other initiatives. It is the first time that the state has treated the media as public policy, as a right of citizenship. Until now, the relationship established has been one of dependence, co-option, or alignment, through the purchase of advertising space, various subsidies or tax incentives.

With the *Ponto de Mídia Livre*, social communication is treated as an essential asset for citizenship and this free and autonomous communication needs to be financed via funds dispensed directly by people and the state. It is a new form of media financing: without any commitment to advertising; requiring nothing in exchange. The commitment of the *Ponto de Mídia Livre* is to a democracy of many voices, to polyphony. And nothing more.

Another crack opens.

By connecting *Pontos de Cultura* with *Pontos de Mídia Livre*, we take a step forward. In addition to the production and circulation of culture within communities, we open up a wider cultural diffusion. The magazine *Viração*, produced by young people for young people. *Intervozes*, a news agency that had no voice. *Thyedeá*, a network of Indians from the Northeast of Brazil; *Ocas*, the magazine produced by the homeless in São Paulo. The magazine *Raiz*, in which the popular is classical. Independent blogs, portals, alternative connections, protection of the environment. Community Radio and TV channels spread across the country.

It is still in its infancy, but, with this *ação*, free culture and free communication are coming together and complement each other. Communication exists only because there is culture to be transmitted; culture exists through the act of communicating. Points of reunion. And of mutation.

Pontão (Big *Pontos* – Cultural Hubs)

If the *Ponto de Cultura* is a network within a specific territory, the *Pontão de Cultura* is the node that supports the network. *Pontões* are articulators, enablers and diffusers within the network; they are part of *ações* and act within thematic or territorial spheres. They may cover an artistic genre (*Pontão do Teatro do Oprimido*; *Pontão do Audiovisual*), a target group such as young people, an area of interest such as Agrarian Reform, or a geographical or administrative area. With the *Pontões*, we created intra-network management, a way of finding mechanisms within the network itself, without external agents, relying on the capacity and skills of the participants.

The first *Pontão* was established almost in parallel with the *Pontos*: it was *Navegar Amazônia*, a boat-studio that travels the mouth of the River Amazon. Afterwards came the *Pontões Ação Griô*, *Vídeo nas Aldeias* [an audiovisual project run by indigenous people] and *Mapa da Rede*, which manages and systemises information on the *Pontos* and *Cultura Viva*. There is a *Pontão* dedicated to conflict resolution which supports the dissemination of a culture of *paz* – peace – throughout the network (a *Ponto de Cultura* may also be called a *Ponto de Paz*).

With the *Pontão*, the network can support itself with greater strength, gaining autonomy and boosting internal leadership. Now it is the agents of the *Pontos de Cultura* themselves that feed the network with new ideas, initiatives and *ações*. Effective networks break the relationship of dependence and take one more step on the path to emancipation.

Cultura Viva award

The *Cultura Viva* award was created to strengthen dialogue beyond the network of *Pontos de Cultura*. We created various themes: social technology, culture and education. Through these different categories we can reach the widest variety of agents: state schools, governments, social organisations, businesses, *Pontos de Cultura*, informal groups and individual initiatives. The award is a way of mapping, going beyond the groups already known, thus broadening the dialogue between government and society. The award enables us to systematise practices, concepts and methodologies, to identify that which is most viable in the cultural outputs of communities, in public policies and in the corporate social responsibilities of companies.

It is also a means of recognition and legitimisation:

'For us, it was a challenge, because this is the first time that we have been participants in an award and it turned out successfully.... The recognition through the Cultura Viva award has shown us a little of our reality, how we live in our community, the stories of the Baniwa people of the Alto Rio Negro. With this recognition, we are able to guarantee the recording of our cultural reality for future generations. If we do not record our culture, we are a people without identity and without a history.'

Moisés Baniwa, São Gabriel da Cachoeira, Amazonas

For Dona Valdete da Silva Cordeiro, of the *Meninas de Sinhá*, Belo Horizonte, to receive an award that bestows recognition and appreciation is 'something that changes us and makes us think: about how we began, the difficulties, our hits and misses, about the people who helped us along the way, remembering that we need to grow more, to do more for ourselves and for others.'

Training and incentives are provided to help the awardees develop as a network, including a TV series, which explains the concepts and methodology of the *Cultura Viva* programme. An award that is also cultural mapping.

Means of diffusion

The means by which the the *Cultura Viva* programme communicates is part of its *raison d'être*, as the programme engages in dialogue rather than mere institutional dissemination. In formulating the *Cultura Viva* programme, this preoccupation was present from the outset:

'*Cultura Viva* is, above all, a programme of social mobilisation and enchantment.... The success of the programme involves interaction, the exchange of information and the wide distribution of knowledge.... The means of communication and diffusion need to be shared with all participants in the programme.'

From the outset, we imagined a means of presenting the experiences and initiatives of the *Ponto de Cultura* programme. And *Cultura Ponto a Ponto* (Culture Point to Point) emerged, shown by public TV networks and documenting more than 120 *Pontos de Cultura* by 2009. A radio programme – *Cultura Viva* online radio – was created by the *Pontão Mapa dos Pontos* and made available via a portal, so that people could listen to programmes directly on the Internet or rebroadcast them via local, public or community radio. A series of more than sixty 'inter-programmes' were broadcast on *TV Brasil* and the *Canal Futura* cable channels (up to three minutes long, they were shown in the middle of normal TV schedules). A magazine (*Raiz*) appeared, in partnership with a private publisher, and was sold at newsstands and as an e-magazine via the web.

Three more cable TV programmes were developed: *Ponto Brasil*, *Amálgama Brasil* and *Cidades Invisíveis*. *Ponto Brasil* is a collaborative TV production experience, providing training in the production of original content and narratives, which involved more than a hundred *Pontos de Cultura* as participants in the research, training, experimentation and promotion. *Amálgama Brasil* arose from a partnership between the nationally revered musician and poet Jorge Mautner (who championed the *Ponto de Cultura* programme) and a major Brazilian cinema producer, Luiz Carlos Barreto. They produced a series that goes beyond merely documenting the work of the *Pontos*, promoting interaction between artists and intellectuals: a real 'amalgamation'. *Cidades Invisíveis* started out as a regional production in the state of Minas Gerais, revealing unnoticed details about our cities; it is a collaboration between *Pontos de Cultura* and the state cable TV Channel *Rede Minas*.

Many other initiatives unfolded throughout Brazil: radio programmes; regional TV programmes; newsreels, blogs and murals, and everything else that makes the living culture of Brazil even more alive.

Teia (spider's web)

It was a symbolic decision. The first bringing together of the *Pontos* would have to be in the São Paulo Biennial pavilion. No other place, no other city; it was necessary to start at Brazil's economic, financial and artistic hub.

Teia 2006: 'See yourselves and be seen.' This was the first time the *Pontos de Cultura* could witness themselves as a movement. Before the *Teia*, the *Pontos* were dispersed; afterwards, they had formed themselves into countless groups and forged new relationships.

From the beginning of the programme, I had envisaged a meeting for the *Pontos de Cultura* to see themselves as a network, but before this could happen it was necessary to spin the threads, to sow the seeds. In less than two years the network was set up. At the end of 2005 we took the decision: the meeting of *Pontos de Cultura* would have to take place before the election period, which meant in just a few months' time. The government was going through a major political crisis and we could not risk such an incipient network being dismantled. I had already been through that with the network in Campinas; when the government changed, the *Casas de Cultura* fell away. The network must be consolidated before the elections, there was no other time, the *Pontos de Cultura* had to see each other, and be seen.

And it had to be during the São Paulo Biennial, canon of so-called 'established art' – the icon of cultural trends. All we needed was a few days' gap in the calendar. Art with no defined aesthetic school, coming from the peripheries, be they geographical, aesthetic or social. It was a beautiful sight to see all those *Pontos* entering that enormous building with its modern architectural style.

> *Thus everything was written in one outpouring, rough but real, in this conflict of shattered confrontation of art without heart attack, outside the market, but alive, in the year of grace 2006, by this simple pilgrim of lucky accidents.'*
> 'More or less manifesto', TT Catalão, poet, consultant, and later director of 'Access to Culture' at the Secretariat of Cultural Citizenship

The second *Teia* took place in 2007 at the Palácio das Artes in Belo Horizonte, in the presence of President Lula, with a ceremony in which he presented Brazil's highest cultural honour – the Order of Cultural Merit – to a range of distinguished artists.

The *Teia* is a movement of permanent invention, in which the different see themselves as the same. Its manifesto proclaims that the *Teia* 'advances on the silences that refuse to be perceived – your culture is yours – attack, act – happen … those who are ready are finished'.

In 2006, 3,000 people participated and there were 50,000 visitors over four days. People from every corner of Brazil and beyond. The vast concrete and glass pavilion of the Biennial was invaded by wooden partitions, coloured flags and calico.

The *Teia* is a mixture of enchantment, reflection and organisation. The enchantment comes from the explosion of the *Pontos*, from their pulsating creativity, from their strangeness, from the discovery of points in common, from the artistic presentations. The reflection occurs through the holding of seminars, debates and also by the non-academic forms of sharing knowledge. Each *Teia* has a new transversal theme: 'Culture and Economic Solidarity' in 2006, 'Culture and Education' in 2007 and 'Culture and Human Rights' in 2009. This mixture of people, things and ideas elicits the perception that the *Pontos* can always go further, because, in the words of Gilberto Gil, 'from the conjunction of many points, a line is made, which forms designs and ideas'.

Those who participated in one or all of the *Teias* know what this moment of 'take off' represents. It is an explosion of feelings and reflections, the 'distribution of the sensible' of which the French philosopher Rancière writes. The *Teia* is a moment of cultural, social and political praxis. Not a formal meeting in which delegates hold up their name tags, nor an academic seminar, with specialists and listeners, nor an artistic exhibition or festival conceived by a curator. The *Teia* is a mixture of all this, a little chaotic, but organised. A moment in which we say: 'The ways that we have been recommended up to now do not work for us. We want others.' A subtle process of changing mentalities, which finds its strength in culture.

Teia: people in movement, spinning their story.

Aesthetic interactions

Promoting a culture without limits was always the intention of the *Cultura Viva* programme. In the beginning, it was necessary to sow the seeds, sharpen eyes and ears to perceive those least seen and heard. But remaining only in this dimension would not break barriers. We needed to cross frontiers. My first initiative was to invite the eminent sculptor and curator Emanoel Araújo to create an exhibition. Integrating the *Pontos de Cultura* within the broad cultural panorama of Brazil, the exhibition '*Viva Cultura Viva do Povo Brasileiro*' opened at the Afro-Brazilian Museum in São Paulo in October 2006. In the catalogue, Araújo writes:

> '*To witness the Cultura Viva of the Brazilian people in all its diversity of action and creation really is something unique.... This venture has the same extravagant and anarchic sense as Cultura Viva, in order to be able to symbolically bring together the great halo of permanencies and absences.*'

After that exhibition, the *Cultura Viva* network grew, but a connection was missing between the *Pontos de Cultura* and professional artists. We therefore created a new *ação* called *Interações Estéticas* (Aesthetic Interactions) which offers grants ranging from R$15,000 to R$90,000 [approximately £30,000 at the time]. The aim was to encourage shared creative processes between professional contemporary artists and the *Pontos de Cultura*. An aesthetic interaction that breaks through boundaries between classical art, contemporary art and popular art. Without such an initiative, *Pontos de Cultura* would have continued to be circumscribed by stereotypes and prejudices. We have advanced. Contemporary art is art produced live, wherever it comes from, whoever it is produced by. Classical art is not culture, it is a form of instruction or study to achieve excellence, but it is not culture in itself: it is method. What is popular in one epoch may be elite and classical in another age.

Erudition, studying, reading are without doubt indispensable. Without erudition, perhaps the song of the *Uirapuru* [an Amazonian bird of mythical status] would never have become a symphonic poem through the work of the Brazilian composer Heitor Villa-Lobos. But he too learned music under adverse conditions. His father, Raul Villa-Lobos, an employee of the National Library, taught him the cello by improvising with a viola, and he learned to play guitar in popular *choro* groups. Only later did he compose symphonies. The opposite may also happen. Tom Jobim was a classically trained musician before he composed *bossa novas*. The aim of *Interações Estéticas* is not to superimpose specific art forms, but to provide different, multiple ways of creating a work of art.

In 2008, I commissioned an exhibition from the artist and curator Bené Fonteles to coincide with the third *Teia* in Brasília. With its title of '*Neither Classical nor Popular*', the exhibition's aim was to reveal proximities, breaking down barriers in that search for a universal

Brazilian identity that the polymath Mário de Andrade refers to as 'our culture in progress'. In the exhibition catalogue, Bené Fonteles writes:

'Making art is transforming the ordinary into the extraordinary. This is what the Brazilian people do with their surprising creativity when coming up with strategies for survival, from the oca indigenous dwelling to the senzala slave houses, from the shack to the slum. Hélio Oiticica found the inspiration to create his 'Penetráveis' [installation works the viewer experiences by entering] in the emergency architecture of the favelas of Rio de Janeiro, and in the clothing and movements of sambistas to make his 'Parangolés' [wearable sculptures or sculptural costumes], with which he dressed his dancers, dancing within their poetic space....

The fragile frontier between what is popular art and classical art is crossed by Oiticica, in the full cultural effervescence of the 1960s. It is his penetrable ' Tropicália', of 1967, which gives its name to the most revolutionary and transgressive movement in Brazilian culture.'

The first *Interações Estéticas* programme selected 90 projects. A rapprochement of distant worlds, sometimes physically close, but totally different from a social, economic and cultural point of view. After this interaction neither artists nor *Pontos* will ever be the same again.

Areté

This *ação* was intended to be a funding programme for *Pequenos Eventos* (Small Events). Over 500 applications arrived from all over Brazil. One hundred and seventy were selected with an investment of R$4 million [approximately £1.3 million at the time].

For such a wide variety of ambitious proposals the name *Pequenos Eventos* was no longer appropriate. I asked for another name to be found. In the indigenous Tupi language, *areté* means 'feast day'. In ancient Greek, it means 'virtue, excellence'. The fusion of two cultures in just one word. *Areté*: the path to perfection in being, a key concept of Western philosophy. *Areté*: a new *ação* of the *Cultura Viva* programme. Events detached from the processes that created them become lost in themselves, but when they are cultivated as part of a process they may lead to new levels of excellence in behaviour and ideas. The word *areté* represents this. For indigenous peoples, this permanent cultivation of 'being' is established by example, through admiration of the deeds of others, by good conduct, not by the simple transmission of rules. In Homeric poems, *áristos* (which comes from *areté*) is he who brings together all qualities, the 'complete human'.

What would the excellent person be? Can we be trained and educated to be excellent?

With the *Ação Areté* we sought to 'mine' other forms of excellence, found in places other than those that form us.

Diálogo entre Aldeias (Dialogue between Villages) proposed dialogues between Tapeba and Xavante Indians, meetings in which indigenous filmmakers (of the Xavante tribe) would exchange experiences with their relatives from the community of Caucaia, in the metropolitan region of Fortaleza in the state of Ceará. Until the 1980s, FUNAI (National Indian Foundation) records indicated that there were no Indians inhabiting the state of Ceará. But the Tapeba people thus condemned to oblivion reclaimed their identities and petitioned for their right to repossess their territory, winning official reclassification as an indigenous people in 1993. *Diálogo entre Aldeias,* therefore, was a pertinent and necessary initiative to place the debate about indigenous Cearense identities on a national platform, initially in alliance with the Xavante Indians from the Southern state of Mato Grosso.

The same process took place with the *Oficinas Lúdicas* (Games Workshops) for children at state schools in the Vale do Café, in southern Rio de Janeiro. Who offers the workshops? A *Ponto de Cultura* in the *favela* of Rocinha. The proposal is to connect with children through prose and games. A map-game in the form of a path in which participants in the game get to know the meanderings of one of the largest *favelas* in Rio de Janeiro. *Rocinha Lúdica* offers a counterpoint to the stereotypical view of violence in the slum. Stories to be discovered, games to be shared between adults and children. What is the meaning of this event? 'By playing, we learn about ourselves and about others; by playing, we create links between people, groups and places; by playing, we join together strands of history.' Before becoming a *favela*, Rocinha was a *quilombo* – a community of slaves who liberated themselves – as is the *Quilombo de Pinheiral,* near Vassouras – and both of them are *Pontos de Cultura.* They meet.

Some events focused on study and practice, as in the *Confluências TecnoCulturais: desafios e perspectivas* (Techno-Cultural Confluences: challenges and prospects), a proposal from a *Pontão* at the Federal University of Minas Gerais. In contrast, *Rios de Encontro* – Rivers of Encounter – was a cultural forum based in the region of Carajás in the state of Pará, because it is a zone of conflict which has witnessed the guerrilla war of Araguaia and the massacre of the landless workers of Eldorado dos Carajás. *Marias Brasilianas: a arte do fio* (Brazilian Marias: the art of thread) brought together weavers from Olhos D'Água and the Vale do Jequitinhonha with lacemakers from the Northeast and Dumont embroiderers. The event was drenched in the cultural wealth and diversity of the communities involved, be they the participants of the *Pontos de Cultura* or women artisans, creating a network of cultural meanings upon which common actions can be developed. An exercise in exchange that sought to spread excellence and values. An exercise in *Areté*.

10. THE STATE FROM THE BOTTOM UP

'This newly enunciated world will not be a construction from the top down, like those we see today and deplore, but an edifice whose trajectory will be from the bottom up.'
Milton Santos

When asked about where solutions to the most serious problems caused by 'perverse' globalisation would come from, the Brazilian geographer Milton Santos replied: 'from scarcity, and those at the bottom'. He was not referring to the struggle for survival that borders on barbarity, and thus precludes choice or the cultivation of thought, but the scarcity that lives side by side with abundance. Scarcity that results from inequality.

'Deep down, the question of scarcity appears again as central. Those "at the bottom" do not possess the means (material or otherwise) to participate fully in modern mass culture. But their culture, being based on territory, on work, and on daily life, gains the necessary strength to distort, in that place, the impact of mass culture. People together create culture and, alongside it, create an economy of place, a discourse of their place, a politics of place. This neighbourhood culture attaches value to the experience of scarcity and the experience of cohabitation and solidarity at the same time.'
Milton Santos, *Por uma Outra Globalização* (For Another Globalisation), p. 144

Through the *Ponto de Cultura* programme we are attempting a partnership with those 'at the bottom', who have scant resources but no scarcity of ideas.

Brazil does not lack thinkers to point to different paths. Milton Santos, José Bonifácio de Andrada, Mário de Andrade, Josué de Castro, Paulo Freire, Celso Furtado and Darcy Ribeiro, among others. We do not suffer from scarcity of natural resources, or history, or ideas, although our natural resources have been sold off since the beginning of colonisation, serving only a restricted class, transferring wealth abroad and gaining little value at home. Our history has also been hidden; our ideas for change and transformation, scorned. But from 'the bottom', a new Brazil is emerging.

'I hear the voices
I see the colours
I feel the steps
of another Brazil that is coming.'

Eighty years ago, Gilberto Freyre had already perceived the movement that is germinating all over the country. For a long time we thought that change in the social order and in the character of the state would occur through a change in economic structure. Culture, as a reflection of the economic environment, would change afterwards. Thus, revolutionaries and reformists directed their thoughts and energies towards the field of political economy, since everything else would come as a consequence. We were mistaken. The structural changes did not occur and our conservative modernisations have only reinforced old models. In other lands, where there have been changes in the economic and social order without a corresponding change in mentalities and values, states have collapsed like the walls they built.

So we must start again, understanding that economics, ethics and aesthetics are inseparable. Culture is at the same time the product and the vector of society. Therefore, culture must be the basis of any historical change in our state of civilisation. Was it not through culture that the *conquistadores* imposed their domination? In Cuzco, the seat of the Inca Empire, the Spanish governor's palace was built directly on top of the Inca palace; the Catholic churches used the same stones and were located in the same place as the Aztec temples. They understood that the symbolic battle is as important as – or more than – the military one. Over the ruins of destroyed palaces, they erected the symbols of the emerging power.

Thinking about culture in the construction of new public space involves breaking down hierarchies and building new legitimacies. A public policy of access to culture has to go beyond a mere offer of participatory arts activities, cultural venues and products; it needs to be extended in a broad sense, expressed in a programme that respects the autonomy of social agents, strengthens their leading role and generates social empowerment; culture to bring different forces together, rapprochement in order that the different perceive themselves as being close in essence. Culture that encourages, unites and makes possible. This has been the principal objective of the *Cultura Viva* programme: to seek a culture that liberates.

We seek to enter the flow of life and activate a process that facilitates change. Change in the social, economic and political order, forged from culture. A bottom-up state presupposes a change in thinking and values. We must upend the temptation to plan in committees, ignoring real life. The path that we are treading with the *Ponto de Cultura* programme is one of less structure and more flow. Rather than doing for, we seek to do with. To make available, rather than to impose.

By inverting the approach and giving potency to what already exists, we have sought a new practice, built on enchantment, magic and art, valuing the initiatives of those who *do* and wish to continue *doing*. This different form of relationship between the state and society opens a gap, a small crack towards a new paradigm of the state.

Underlying the partnership between state and civil society is the principle that it is the people who make culture and not the state. An idea simple to put into words, but difficult to put into practice. The state continues to have an irreplaceable role: to ensure a wide-ranging public policy that covers everyone, guaranteeing rights of access, above all to those historically excluded from established culture or from the culture of the market. Without this presence of the state, there is no public space and democracy disappears, well-intentioned though the localised actions may be, as is often the case with NGOs.

From an emancipatory perspective, it is incumbent on the state to potentiate society, connecting its initiatives via networks, increasing the capacity for reflection and creation. It is society that does this. We do not *create* a *Ponto de Cultura*. For example, the *Maracatu Leão Coroado*, in Igaraçu (Pernambuco), which is a *Ponto*, has been active for 150 years and will continue to exist regardless of the state. What has happened is the *legitimation* of this action by the state. With it, a new relationship of equality and respect has been established, with non-authoritative financial support and dialogue.

Throughout the history of humanity from Ancient Egyptian times until today, it has been an intrinsic characteristic of the state to centralise energies and resources; and to impose set paths. And so an ideology spreads, naturalising its own thinking, standards and conduct until we believe that the dominant way is the only way to live.

If the process of concentrating energies and resources generated wealth (which was appropriated by a minority), it also prevented the expansion of people's creative energies. Today, this drive towards private accumulation has been translated into the operations of international bodies and councils, which impose standards and prevent the release of people's creative energies, for example, through the control of patents, copyright without balanced rights, and unfair standards in trade.

The move towards globalisation of the planet has been a feature of human history since humans left the African savannah. But globalisation as it presents itself to us today is nothing more than the expansion of the interests of large corporations and the expropriation of natural and human resources. The *Ponto de Cultura* movement, and many others, arose to find gaps in this process. And, when they find them, they open them wide. Within the gaps, a new kind of state may be exercised, one that *disposes*: makes available. A state that disposes is not the same as a state that *distributes* – a necessary process in some circumstances, but still inefficient because it does not share decision-making. Even a mass of people in possession of distributed resources struggle to make their voices heard against the negotiating power of the monopolist atop his stockpile. We need a new kind of state that starts to open up and listen, becoming more permeable to the movements of society, to collective wills.

Simply listening to demands is insufficient. We must listen to how to do things, ensuring autonomy, respecting leadership, empowering. We need a variety of intermediary networks that connect through affinities, territories, audiences, languages and interests. Through networks, society gains strength. A state may learn to converse with social movements in a different way, not as controller or provider, but as an organisational partner, included within the network.

This change in the ways the state and the people relate to each other involves modifying everything, down to the smallest gestures of top management and the daily behaviour of bureaucrats. The administrator has to learn to speak to the hip hop artist. Sometimes angry, acting out revulsion and non-conformity, finding it difficult to present his or her demands clearly, unable to grasp legal hindrances, the hip hop artist encounters a world of barriers. It is necessary to understand that this kind of conduct occurs because nothing has ever been offered to her or him, only disrespect, a lack of rights and invisibility – and also to her or his parents, grandparents and great-grandparents. When a person or a nation is maltreated, their reaction to conformism is likely to be rage and tension. A little comprehension and patience are essential, throughout the lengthiest of dialogues and the shortest of interchanges between state and society.

Neither the interventionist and bureaucratic state – providing and populist – or the minimal state – which frees itself of responsibility for its people, placing itself at the disposal of market concentration – takes into account the needs of society. Despite all the rhetoric in defence of a reduction in the size of the state, which has been heard in Brazil and elsewhere, the principal result of this discourse has been the concentration of wealth.

In Brazil, between 1994 and 2004, there was a rise in the total amount of tax collected in the order of 10 per cent of GDP. These were years of concentration and not liberation of the resources produced by society. Concentrated and distributed to a small minority – 20,000 families becoming the borrowers of practically the entire national debt. In little more than ten years, the Brazilian state passed over R$1.4 trillion, or 6 per cent of GDP, to these few. By contrast, the *Bolsa Família* credit programme, which ensured a minimum income for 11 million families, involves spending 0.6 per cent of GDP. As was to be expected, the press and intellectuals at the service of the dominant system have directed much more criticism towards the programme of distribution of income to 11 million families than to the mechanisms that have allowed the private appropriation of public wealth for the benefit of 20,000. Maybe because these families are their families.

For a Living State

The *Ponto de Cultura* appears as an interstice in this process of concentration, but it has already shown results which point to a state that aims at being neither the minimum nor the maximum but efficient and in tune with its people. Lighter in its touch and, at the same time, wide ranging. The sociologist Manuel Castells talks of the aim to create a 'network state' that combines administrative principles such as: flexibility; administrative transparency; decentralisation, shared sovereignty and responsibility; coordination of democratically established rules; participation by the citizen, above all the excluded; technological modernisation; valuation of civil servants; and feedback and assessment that allow learning and the correction of mistakes.

The theory of the *Ponto de Cultura* seeks to value and exercise social responsibility, pushing back against the tendency towards conformism and the standardisation of ways of thinking and acting, with the market as the absolute god.

Our world is one of highly interdependent but at the same time distanced and isolated parts. On the one hand, there is the world of systems (state, market), on the other, the world of life (people). The world of systems, highly structured, is regulated through the mediators of money (market) or power (state). Without doubt, the world of life ends up contaminated by money and power, and it would be easy to attribute all social ills to them. But it is not so simple.

Mediation, or regulation, of the world of life can be achieved through solidarity, affection, or compassion; but also by less positive means, such as hate, envy, or vengeance. Some indigenous societies find their *raison d'être* in vengeance, in hatred between races or tribes, vendettas or blood feuds that encode individuals' behaviour in a never-ending cycle of retaliation. The *Ponto de Cultura* seeks to be an alternative point of mediation between life and systems. Money transforms everything into merchandise, including our dreams, and power is strong; money and power make things so much stronger, they commodify life. When things reveal themselves to be so strong, I always resort to a magnificent verse by Carlos Drummond de Andrade, which I repeat like a mantra:

'Things are so strong,
but I am not things,
and I revolt.'

The human necessity not to become a thing, to break through alienation and emancipate oneself, even when forcibly contained, always comes to the fore at some point. It is difficult to make it germinate, but sometimes it blossoms.

In these neoliberal times, the rule has been to analyse societies by cold macroeconomic indicators: accounting data, the vitality of the stock market, growth or recession, risk indices and AAA or downgraded credit ratings. If we analysed GDP per capita between 1988 and 2008 in Brazil, we would definitely reach the conclusion that we had stagnated and stood still in this race. But if we look further, with a little more sensitivity, perhaps we can see that major changes occurred. Life expectancy increased, child mortality fell, the AIDS epidemic was kept reasonably well under control, society is more active. In the poor peripheries of the large metropolises or in the small municipalities in the so-called corners of Brazil, it is possible to see that a new country is emerging. Jardim Ângela, one of the regions of greatest social vulnerability in Greater São Paulo, has managed to reduce its astronomical homicide rate by 70 per cent. The engineering that managed this improvement in quality of life was the social network established by those 'at the bottom', through scarcity, through the work of the people of Jardim Ângela themselves.

It was exactly this pulsating Brazil that I sought to identify and potentiate with the *Pontos de Cultura*. There is still a long way to go. Despite its transformational capacities, culture is not perceived as a priority: in society, in the economy or in the state. Through the *Ponto de Cultura* programme communities present a new way of seeing themselves and being seen. When a child sees him- or herself reflected in the mirror and recognises that the image is theirs, they are ready to establish relationships outside the confinements of the maternal circle; by extrapolating this to society, we see that the dominant system impedes this essential right to full realisation of the human personality. Withdrawing the right to a mirror means preventing adult communication from being established between people and social groups. Hence, it becomes easier to dominate, concentrate energies, impose, destroy the planet, exploit others.

The only element common to all *Pontos de Cultura*, the multimedia studio, is the mirror offered to every *Ponto*. Recognising itself in the mirror, society may start to overcome this process of alienation; leaving the stage of 'nobodyness', as Darcy Ribeiro defines it, and entering the stage of 'I am', through which we discover and emancipate ourselves. The basis for this new political culture is the reclamation of the idea of the common good. What is the common good? Simple and vital elements like water, air, the environment and culture. There may be others, but let's stick with these. Water, environment and culture have been turned into commodities, like land, health and education. The air? Not yet, but it would not be a surprise to see 'pure mountain air' offered for retail in the near future. Can it be that this appropriation of the common good is part of human nature? Must we passively live with this commodification of life?

Reclaiming the common good as an essential element of culture and politics is to begin to develop politics from values, rather than from interests. Maybe this was one of the problems of institutional politics in the twentieth century, and which is prompting such agony in the twenty-first (be it in Brazil or anywhere else in the world). Politics has become a means of defending interests. To move from 'interests' to 'self-interested' is a tiny step. This is what we are seeing today: self-interested politicians defending increasingly narrow interests. And the sense of the common good disappears.

The quest for substantive and effective democracy lies in the redefinition of politics, which needs to be restored to its purpose of being a mediation between people, between life and systems.

With the *Pontos de Cultura*, we exercise an alternative social and political practice, seeking within real problems the solutions for a state that learns to fraternise with its people and is thus shaped in their image.

Despite experiencing moments of uncertainty, the world looks to Brazil with considerable hope. Darcy Ribeiro, in his book-letter-will *O Povo Brasileiro* (The Brazilian People), calls us the 'New Rome', a meeting of civilisations, peoples and cultures. We are new peoples, making ourselves anew.

> '*A new civilisation, mixed-race and tropical, proud of itself. Happier because it has suffered more. Better, because it incorporates more humanity within itself. More generous, because it is open to living in harmony with all races and all cultures and because it lies in the most beautiful and enlightened province on Earth.*'

Mário de Andrade predicted in the early twentieth century, without any sense of euphemism: 'We will be the civilisation of the third millennium.' We Brazilians are no better or worse than other peoples; we have problems like every other nation, but we have also found new solutions. Beneath the rotten institutions there are signs of a new democracy. For this reason, we are 'unhiding' Brazil, looking at ourselves and seeing that within this process are the seeds of a new form of state: a Living State.

POINTS OF CONTACT
An afterword from the UK

'Visibility is such a key element ...'
David Slater, Entelechy Arts

In July 2009, People's Palace Projects organised a visit to the UK by Célio Turino, shortly after his book *Ponto de Cultura* was first published in Brazil. The visit included a discussion on the *Ponto de Cultura* programme, hosted by the Brazilian Embassy. Turino met Mick Elliott, Director of Culture at the Department for Culture, Media and Sport, and then Moira Sinclair, Executive Director, Arts Council England London; the proposal for a cultural knowledge exchange was formed and *Points of Contact* began the following year.

Points of Contact/Pontos de Contato was created to increase the skills and capacity of arts organisations, policy makers and funders to realise the full potential of dynamic and transformative cultural actions that emerge from and engage with diverse communities: to build new networks of cultural understanding and creativity between Brazil and the UK. The ongoing project is a partnership between Arts Council England, the British Council, the Department for Culture, Media and Sport (DCMS), People's Palace Projects (PPP) and the Ministry of Culture in Brazil.

'Culture has the capacity to transform people's lives, making possible a diverse exchange of knowledge and practices. Our policy has been to stimulate the flux, the flow, the fusion of cultural points in Brazil. We believe that by making an interaction with Points of Contact in the UK, we can strengthen the forces of integration between us all.'
Célio Turino, introduction to the programme for the *Points of Contact* seminar, Southbank Centre, October 2010

Over 150 British and Brazilian arts organisations have participated in the *Points of Contact* exchange programme since 2010. Some of them concentrated their learning experience during the time they spent together at each other's companies and in each other's countries. Others have formed lasting bonds which have resulted in collaborative projects: such as Entelechy Arts (UK) and *Casa das Fases* (Brazil).

Based at The Albany in Deptford, Entelechy is a participatory arts company that has produced twenty years of quietly transformational practice with people of all ages and abilities – elders, people in care and residential homes, younger people and those with learning difficulties and complex disabilities. It creates theatre, dance, video events and performances. Entelechy's ability to couple imaginative, daring arts work with listening and empathy, connecting people who can be profoundly isolated from their communities and unlocking creative energies, has earned them enormous respect. These qualities made them a strong candidate for the first phase of an exchange aiming to inspire and fortify arts organisations who want to transform lives and celebrate communities beyond the mainstream.

Casa das Fases (The House of the Ages) is a *Ponto de Cultura* based in the city of Londrina, Paraná, in the interior of Southern Brazil. Working almost exclusively with men and women over the age of sixty-five, after twenty-five years they are still producing radical and experimental work that has been presented across Brazil and beyond. When the Brazilian Ministry of Culture was asked to nominate a partner for Entelechy, there was no hesitation.

'They announce themselves with music, and then open their boxes of memories, like little theatres in which they perform their stories for an audience of one. For a few brief moments, a cardboard box hung around their necks becomes a stage and a museum. The scenography and costumes are lovingly made in miniature, with little toys, photos, dolls, crêpe paper and fabric ... Full of music, stories and verses, they win over the streets. And rediscover themselves: "This group is like my family, since I've been widowed," says a white-haired old lady.'
Célio Turino, *Ponto de Cultura*, 'Little Boxes of Memories'[1]

'Motorists double take at the large group of people moving like a shoal down the back streets of New Cross Gate. Distinguished men in suits being pushed along in wheelchairs, a young woman with a bicycle, people of all ages. There are people from just around the corner and people from far away: a dancer from Minneapolis, a writer from Bradford, musicians, poets, producers, a man pushing his mother.'[2]

David Slater, Entelechy's Artistic Director, documents *The Deptford Project* in September 2011, which built long-term relationships with older people living in residential homes, uncovering and rekindling artistic skills and ambitions, and encouraging its participants to journey

---

1. A chapter in Célio Turino's original book, replaced in the English edition by this Afterword.
2. David Slater's blog at Entelechy Arts. http://davidaslater.wordpress.com/2011/09/27/the-triumphant-procession/

out into the world again with a story, poem, a song or dance. The final performance was to take place in a community hall half a mile from the care home; should they hire a minibus? No: 'we will walk down the street'. Remembering the ladies of *Casa das Fases*, Slater describes how Entelechy bought parasols 'and nearly caused a few road traffic accidents ... Passers-by couldn't stop staring at these seemingly incongruous relationships.' The spectators were watching 'the theatre of the journey'. And in their togetherness the participants found agency, 'moving with common purpose down the street'. Interviewed in 2013, Slater points to this moment of 'triumphant procession' as just one example of the ways Brazil continues to emerge in Entelechy's work today.[3]

David Slater travelled to Brazil in March 2010 as part of a group of twenty-six UK artists, funders, policy makers, and arts workers. The thirteen arts organisations who participated ranged from large institutions (The Sage Gateshead, Barbican, Royal Shakespeare Company, National Theatre Wales, Southbank Centre) to smaller companies specialising in engagement with a particular group (Entelechy, Contact – Manchester's famous theatre company for young people, The Lawnmowers learning-disabled theatre company, Freedom Studios in Bradford – born from the pioneering Asian Theatre School) or in digital arts work (B3 Media, Watershed/iShed); from network organisations (DaDa Deaf and Disabled Arts, Voluntary Arts Network) to individual Fellows on the Clore Cultural Leadership Programme (Joe Hallgarten and Ariane Koek). To give a spread of perspectives on arts policy and funding, the group included representatives from DCMS, Arts Council England, British Council's Brazil team, Culture Liverpool, London 2012, and two independent Foundations with a strong interest in arts and social justice, the Calouste Gulbenkian Foundation UK and Paul Hamlyn Foundation.

Beginning in São Paulo, the exchange gave an overview of some of Brazil's established arts and social institutions (*SESC São Paulo – Serviço Social do Comércio*, and the bank-funded *Itaú Cultural*), the legacy of 1960s radicalism (*Teatro Oficina*) and more recent government investment in revealing hidden voices (the Afro-Brazilian Museum), before visiting some of Rio's extraordinary *favela*-based NGOs that produce life-changing arts work with people living amidst extreme social crisis. In Fortaleza, Northeastern Brazil, the UK artists were welcomed to the 2010 *Teia* by their exchange partners. The party

3. Interview with David Slater on 18 July 2013.

then divided, as the Brazilian artists took their UK partners back to *Pontos de Cultura* ranging from the urban environments of Rio (*Palavras Visíveis, Spectaculu*) and São Paulo (*Bolha de Sabão*) to Porto Nacional in Brazil's interior (*Tambores de Tocantins*), to the rich cultural landscape of Brazil's Northeastern states, so lovingly depicted by Turino in the first sections of this book (*Graõs de Luz e Griôs* in Lençóis, *Teatro Vila Velha* in Salvador, *Orquestra Sertão* in Arcoverde, *Grupo Bongar* in Olinda, *Nos Trilhos do Teatro* in Teresina).

And this was only the start. Since 2010, PPP has supported more than 75 Brazilian and 90 UK participants to visit each other's countries in artistic exchanges, and hosted meetings and discussions for Brazilian visitors with over 70 other UK arts organisations.

'It was completely transformative, those three weeks [in March 2010]. It allowed you to go in completely raw, naked, and allow any possibility; to give you the confidence to trust your intuition and an intuitive way of working.'
David Slater

'A relationship of affection. Stopping to hear another person's story is a very important thing.'
Fabrício Borges, Coordinator, *Casa das Fases*

Entelechy's pairing with *Casa das Fases* is still vibrant three and a half years later. Since March 2010, *Casa das Fases* and Entelechy have met four more times: twice in Brazil, once in the UK and once in Denmark. Members have stayed in regular contact, through modern and more traditional means. Skype and email communication is frequent.

'Everyone's individual letters and mementos are gently folded into a nest of coloured tissue paper tied with a skein of red wool. All week we have been playing with words. How do we express our dreams? What secrets do we share? How do we parcel up packets of ourselves for transportation to Brazil? We wrap scents and objects together with the folded texts.... Theatre creates this space for a re-imagining. The anguished: "what will become of me?" has the possibility of being transformed into the excitement and curiosity of: "what will become of me?" That's the thrill of the project. This shared imagining between minds and bodies 6,020 miles apart. "What might?" asks Antonio in Shakespeare's play [The Tempest]. So the adventure begins. What might?'[4]

---

4.   David Slater's blog at Entelechy Arts. http://davidaslater.wordpress.com/2011/07/17/letters-to-londrina/

The two now talk of each other as 'sister companies'. They use the language of flirtation: 'we're just walking out together, checking in'. David is clear that it is not a rose garden: 'There was and is tension'. The two companies' relationships with their company members are very different. *Casa das Fases* place a high value on professional discipline, and company members have been sacked for not attending rehearsal, while Entelechy's relationships with participants are 'more of a negotiation, because we're interested in working with people in moments of transition in their lives'. And things get fiery – 'sweet old ladies? No way! You soon smash through the "I will play the part of the eighty-year old for you" façade. But they draw strength and confidence from seeing themselves reflected in the other. 'As the next part of the relationship, we want to find a place where some of their company and some of our company can live together for three to four weeks, and lock the doors and make something together....'

New connections

In July 2010, Entelechy watched members of their own company walking out with their stories hung around their necks, to be performed to passers-by at the Southbank Centre. Wishing to unlock the stories of old and young people with profound disabilities, which had to be told in other ways than by a live narrator, Entelechy has recruited a team of artists to create *Little Boxes of Memories*, a collection of multisensory installations that communicate individual memories through the gently silken texture of fur, the sounds and vibrations of speakers, small objects and artefacts, distinctive colours and evocative scents. Slater says the project has connected 'artists, museum teams, teachers, adult social care teams, multidisciplinary health teams, local volunteers, and older Londoners'. He is wryly driven: 'Still obsessing with the challenge of embedding work into the fabric of our communities.'[5] In its newest incarnation, with support from the Heritage Lottery Fund, the project will reach beyond Entelechy's team to work with Lewisham Hospital, and will become a part of the Museum of London's collection in 2015. 'What excites me about it is that beyond us there are now tangible products. It's not us; it's the Museum of London's education team. It's not us; it's the elder care team in Lewisham. It's this external validation [that gives affirmation].'

---

5.   David Slater's blog at Entelechy Arts. http://davidaslater.wordpress.com/2013/05/12/a-procession-of-tables-part-one/

Connections made through *Points of Contact* have resulted in a series of collaborative or internationally inspired UK projects. Entelechy, *Casa das Fases* and Freedom Studios are collaborating with a new project, *The Home*, exploring modern experiences of old age and culminating in site-specific theatre productions in London and Bradford in 2013 and 2014. The Lawnmowers and *Orquestra Sertão*, a learning-disabled music group in Brazil's Northeast, performed together in one of the UK's *Unlimited* commissions for the 2012 Cultural Olympiad, *Boomba Down the Tyne*. In PPP's *Rio Occupation* project, commissioned by Rio de Janeiro State Culture Secretariat, thirty Rio artists lived with co-producer Battersea Arts Centre for a month in summer 2012, were hosted by fifteen London organisations, and created forty-five live performances and three exhibitions across eleven London boroughs. And a conversation about training for employment in creative organisations for young people, which began between the Ministry of Culture and Arts Council England in July 2010, has flowered with partnership support from the British Council into a relationship between The Backstage Centre, Creative & Cultural Skills' training facility at High House Production Park in Thurrock, and centres for arts training in Rio and Bahia.

Ongoing collaborative projects are just one way of demonstrating the impact of international exchange. Alongside the performances and moments of intimate human interaction, the experiences of *Points of Contact* have inspired individuals, organisations and institutions to consider other ways of being.

'The Brazilian experience has forced me to cut through the language of bureaucracy here in the UK and understand my art once again in relation to people and not exclusively to that of funding institutions and quotas.'
Madani Younis, Freedom Studios, March 2010

'The experience has inspired me to be more disciplined, more strategic in my own practice.'
Sérgio Vaz, poet and cultural producer, Cooperifa, March 2012

'The experience [of exchange] has re-energised us as a company. It has given us the courage to re-imagine ourselves; the courage to place the human at the centre of all that we do.... In London, we have been uncovering our own backyards; meeting invisible and isolated groups of people, in forgotten parts of our communities, desperate for connection, recognition, and new experience.'
David Slater, *Points of Contact* seminar, Southbank Centre, October 2010

Through the programme, large and small organisations have experienced the work of *Pontos* such as *AfroReggae*, *Nós do Morro* and *Crescer e Viver*, all of which embed social care at the heart of their institutions. Social workers, psychiatrists and therapists work alongside artists and producers to ensure a holistic approach to socially engaged art. Such encounters have raised questions and ideas about UK methodologies for engaging people in the arts: the exchange has energised and deepened participants' personal sense of mission and values, helping them to find expanded visions or new methodologies for their organisations' practices of engagement and cultural citizenship.

> *'In the UK we need a complete change if we want to make it easier for marginalised groups and communities to have their rightful place at the cultural table – for me Points of Culture is a good starting point.'*
> Geraldine Ling, The Lawnmowers Independent Theatre, October 2010

> *'The visit turned into a profound opportunity for me to re-evaluate and consider not only my professional values and structures but my personal architecture of beliefs and motivations and the points where professional and personal intersect. So the visit has had an impact on me which will, I know, have a lasting effect which will change my behaviour in different spheres of my life and my sense of purpose.'*
> UK participant in the *Points of Contact* exchange, March 2010

> *'It's a transformation (of conceptualisation) from "access to culture" to "the right to cultural expression".'*
> UK participant in *Points of Contact* seminar, Southbank Centre, October 2010

Shân Maclennan, Head of Learning and Participation at Southbank Centre, spoke movingly at the launch of the Cultural Learning Alliance, in late 2010, of the revelation of Brazil's social NGOs and her desire to embed cultural work not in purpose-built arts centres but at the heart of community centres serving a variety of needs – medical clinics, social work, play – recognising culture as an essential part of the fabric of life. Contact Theatre returned to the UK expressing renewed purpose to continue and expand their focus on North Manchester, an underserved area whose young people did not travel to their building. The director of Rio's Centro Cultural Banco de Brazil came away from The Albany inspired to re-imagine CCBB's community engagement. The Lawnmowers' connections with *AfroReggae* (funded by Paul Hamlyn Foundation as part of PPP's separate youth leadership programme,

Cultural Warriors) supported the company's learning-disabled artists to branch out into drumming, and they now describe themselves as an arts hub rather than a theatre company. They aspire to become a *Pontão* for the Northeast of England, connecting Brazilian points of culture and resistance to oppression with their network of UK social organisations. There are UK-UK connections and collaborations, too.

'Strong personal and institutional relationships across the UK participants have been formed, and these are generating supportive peer networks and mentoring, and new collaborations to take forward practice and organisational change inspired by the learning in Brazil. Smaller organisations are mentoring larger ones, and vice versa, and many have found new national and international profile through their involvement overall.'
Points of Contact, first phase report by Kate Tyndall, 2010

Ritual as a form where you can place your feelings

'With a smile on my face and lightness in my soul, I bid farewell to Casa das Fases. But first there is cake, biscuits, tea and fruit juice, for this is how they receive visitors.'
Célio Turino, *Ponto de Cultura*, 'Little Boxes of Memories'

'Of course we have always tried to listen to the voices of our participants. Now we've thrown away the flipchart, and swapped it for rice and chicken. So planning and policy-making is increasingly fixed over communal meals. Our members contribute both ideas and food; it reconnects us with the domestic and the everyday. And this has dramatically increased people's capacity for agency – their ability to articulate, to champion, to advocate for their practice. Our seventy-year-olds said "We want to meet the funders". And so far, over the last six months, they've raised £65,000.'
David Slater, *Points of Contact* seminar, Southbank Centre, October 2010

Interviewed in 2013, Slater returns to the power of social rituals, describing how Entelechy placed them at the centre of their own relationships and creative processes. On his return from Londrina, the company bought a wooden family dining table on eBay. Now it sits at the centre of the office – 'we bought a Brazilian tablecloth for it'. The table has opened up new dialogues and bred a confidence to reinvent relationships. When they wanted to talk to the Council's Adult Social Care team about a possible new project, 'we invited the Lewisham team not to a meeting, but to eat strawberries and croissants and drink coffee with us. This ritual unlocked something. [Instead of pitching] we talked about ideas together. It's the Brazilian way – it's a liminal space.'

Ritual as 'a form in which you can place your feelings' also shapes Entelechy's programme of Twenty-First Century Tea Dances. At one such tea dance in early 2012, entitled *Storm in a Teacup*, elders and young people performed snatches of *The Tempest* amidst filmed interviews with local people about heads of families whose authority had slipped away: fathers and daughters, fraternal betrayals, relationships fractured and repaired. Video images of *Casa das Fases* looked on. And then, of course, the ritual serving of tea and cake, the courteous request for a hand, the ceremonial leading-out, the gradual abandonment to the delight of dancing. '[We think of it as] a basket for very frail older people to talk about loss. But also, possibilities....'

Change makers

For Entelechy and *Casa das Fases*, change comes in taking 'tiny, gentle risks'. Others on the *Points of Contact* programme have questioned themselves and each other through the different contexts in which they have exchanged ideas. But each of them in some way has come back to a central question: How can the artist be a change maker? The unfailingly gentle Slater offers a robust assessment of the political context in which Entelechy asks that question and puts answers into motion. The very question about the role of the artist has been 'reframed' for him by the experience of the exchange and, despite the specificity of Entelechy's work with a particular age group, their learning is echoed across many of the responses from UK participants on the programme. Central to the learning exchange has been a recalibration of the sense of agency which the art produced with diverse communities. 'Co-authorship', the idea of participants as the equal holders of meaning in the artwork, featured in many of the discussions arising out of the exchange, but for Slater it had particular resonance. Slater identifies that within certain UK contexts, 'there is a whole sector of artists helping people to pass the time.... There may be value in that? But [in care homes] these people get taken out of time, out of history. I'm interested in addressing them as historical players. When you're a historical player, you're a maker of change. And change becomes possible in your life. So I want Entelechy to be collaborators, not colluding.'

> *The losses that come with age matter to us when they begin to restrict our agency. Like the freedom acquired in the transition to adulthood it happens in stages. But it happens.*

The practice of art, to whatever degree of skill or ambition, is one form of resistance to that change because ... it confers agency. Through creation, we can act in the world. And there is no age limit on art practice.[6]

Partnerships on the programme were forged in the discovery of common roots for the desire to make change within diverse contexts. There was a powerful recognition of fellowship in a shared struggle between *AfroReggae* from a *favela* in Rio de Janeiro and The Lawnmowers, a theatre company of people with learning disability, in Gateshead. *AfroReggae* discovered the other 'ghetto' in which learning-disabled people live. Hearing the two companies talk about it together in Vigário Geral, Slater found that 'everything was falling into place for me, the things we can't see for looking. If anyone's in a ghetto in the UK, it's the people we warehouse in care homes.... I'm very interested in porousness, "walking through walls", and institutionalised people. How can we transform the day room of the care home into a rehearsal space?' The work is motivated by empathy, not by pity. Entelechy recognises that the community outside loses as much as those inside from our separation, and wants to release the potential of isolated older people to be 'vital elements of the cultural lives of their communities'.

Points of Contact has encouraged and supported a new sense of critical thinking in assessing socially engaged arts policy in the UK through comparing the premises on which it is based and the means of engagement by which it proceeds. Slater, commenting on the Arts Council's plan to commission four projects with people in care homes, identified a new set of challenges arriving with the welcome increase in visibility. In the competition for funds there is a sense that a specialist territory is being staked out, a sector that requires professional knowledge and training to reach across a terrifying expanse of exclusion. He affects bemusement: 'Why on earth would you need to train people to be with people?' He is clear about the threat to artistic practice. 'We seem in the UK to be creating a diluted role for artists.' It is essential that artists resist this dilution. Slater points to Entelechy's circus programme, developed with Vicki Amedume of aerial and circus company Upswing, as an example of practice that refuses to collude with the narrowing of elders' experiences in the name of risk management. Obsessed with avoiding life-changing falls, social care professionals are quick to accept (or impose) limits on what older

---

6. François Matarasso, *Winter Fires: Art and agency in old age,* Baring Foundation, 2012.

people should do. But as a circus practitioner, Vicki has 'reframed walking as a series of falls'. It is the job of the circus artist to convert these falls into performance: and, of course, escape unscathed. So, with active elders, Entelechy and Vicki are playing with circus skills, trapeze and balance. 'Will we be doing fall prevention? Or contemporary circus work?' What they are certainly doing is building physical strength and confidence, offering older people life-affirming experiences and trusting them to make their own decisions about managing the risks. 'We invited some physiotherapists to a dance workshop and they said "how on earth did they [a severely disabled participant] manage that movement?"' Motivation, enjoyment, art, are expanding possibility.

> 'We took some elders to see the Ernesto Neto exhibition at Southbank Centre's Festival Brazil, in summer 2010. It rained. "Ninety-year-olds in the rain!" Their care workers were freaking out. But the elders absolutely loved it. It's just about tiny, gentle risks and the feeling of summer rain.'

How can artists unlock solutions in our uncertain world? What offer can they make? In the context in which Entelechy works, we know that one in six of the UK population is currently aged sixty-five or over, by 2050 it is forecast to be one in four (UK Parliament statistics[7]); and it is clear there will not be 50 per cent more money for their care. Community and social care professionals don't have the answers for the next twenty years, and, for Slater, the ability to create spaces for artists to offer new ideas needs to be part of any state's thinking on social policy and practice.

> Let's ensure our cultural institutions function as porous spaces, engines of social and human transformation that can in turn be transformed.[8]

The Brazilians who came over to the UK on the *Points of Contact* programme visited a range of arts agencies, companies and institutions. They questioned the very essence of how the UK has constructed its arts policy, challenging us to think about whether we have done enough to protect and promote cultural rights as we have laboured to construct and defend our professional arts infrastructure. In Brazil the

---

7. http://www.parliament.uk/business/publications/research/key-issues-for-the-new-parliament/value-for-money-in-public-services/the-ageing-population/
8. See p. 141, *Points Forward*, a declaration made to UK artists and policy makers by the UK participants of the *Points of Contact* programme, October 2010.

focus for our learning was on radical cultural policy that sought to redefine the relationship between the state and the citizen through a focus on a range of community-based practices. In the UK, the Brazilians came to understand that the ways in which we have developed our cultural institutions have allowed us to create structures that can at their best re-invent the role of arts organisations within communities. The Albany in Deptford was the venue for just one of many debates on the programme which demonstrated both the synergy and the differences between the ways in which the UK and Brazil have developed their models of socially engaged arts practices.

Since 1966, in three successive buildings, The Albany in Deptford – Entelechy's base – has been both a home for arts projects and a radical community action centre. The twenty-one companies currently resident there include a complex mix of advocacy and arts organisations for people with learning disabilities, accommodation and support services for vulnerable people including asylum seekers, international theatre companies, writer development and performance poetry agencies, and management support for street traders and theatre companies. If we are looking for the building Shân Maclennan envisaged, that embeds cultural work at the heart of a community centre serving a variety of needs, Deptford is a good place to start. Lewisham Council would agree. The 'dining table' conversation has led to the Council investing in Entelechy and The Albany to pilot a different approach to day care services. *Meet Me At The Albany* is a new initiative that aims to deliver social care in an arts centre, using arts activity as the centre of community activity, alongside other sorts of provision. 'Don't go to a day centre. Go to an arts centre. It's not specialists, it's artists,' says Slater. The Albany describes the pilot:

> *'Every Tuesday, the Albany café will be full of older people, some with substantial needs, some more active, all having lunch, some just watching, some engaged – each to their own. There will also be a cross-disciplinary team of artists, health sector, staff, families and volunteers – so it should be busy. There will be tea and coffee and biscuits too. It really is a pioneering programme that aims to have a transformative effect on adult social care provision in the borough and beyond and if we get it right we would love it to run and run.'*
> The Albany, 2013

From the autumn of 2013, People's Palace Projects is working with a range of partners to nurture projects that continue to grow out of the exchange of ideas from *Points of Contact*. Marcus Faustini visited the UK in March 2012: his youth networks project, *Agência de Redes para a Juventude*, has inspired a major UK venture. Led by Battersea Arts Centre and Contact, in association with PPP and with support from the Calouste Gulbenkian Foundation, *The Agency* is adapting Faustini's methodology to create a project that gives young people the tools, support and networks they need to take an active role within their community. Starting in Battersea and Manchester, then growing in scale, *The Agency* will recruit 300 young people over two years and use artistic devising processes to develop their skills as producers. The aim is to end the initial two years' work in 2015 with both a celebratory festival and a robust, replicable model of participatory arts practice for social transformation that can be offered to other arts and community organisations across the UK.

In the course of PPP's contact with Brazil, we have seen UK practitioners whose personal sense of mission has been renewed and fortified by encounters with Brazilian projects. Expanding the exchange programme beyond the *Pontos de Cultura*, we have continued to focus on projects that embody the deep-seated engagement in their communities that Célio Turino describes. Together we have met people who may lack social, financial or even physical security, but who choose to engage with art because it offers them tools to make meaning in their lives and increase their sense of themselves as agents. These are not simply Brazilian issues. A network of UK practitioners who make work together with communities have begun to build a new solidarity, in a conversation that values their work without feeling a pressure to avoid any taint of instrumentalism.

In the face of Brazil's instability, we have sharpened our appreciation of the strong structures the UK has built in its seven decades of public funding for the arts; and reminded ourselves of what can be achieved when a large cultural institution makes a commitment to reframe its outreach, its participation, as real social engagement.

For People's Palace Projects, the strongest finding of this continuing programme is its affirmation of the value of exchange itself. If the recognition of ourself in the mirror is the first step to participation in the world, then the recognition of ourself in the other – the making of connections that reinforce a deep understanding of the value of art and culture in our lives – is a powerful source of the energy and belief we all, as humans and artists, need. It nourishes our endeavour to go on exploring the new, in the confidence that we can make positive change.

An exchange trip is a moment of reflection. We hear the voices around us anew, and know that our own is heard.

Rosie Hunter with Poppy Spowage

Points Forward

A manifesto presented by the UK and Brazilian artists who participated in the *Points of Contact* exchange in 2010

We propose a clear mission for government and civil society to promote and protect cultural rights for all UK citizens.

We expect that Arts Council England's mission – Great Art for Everyone – will be strengthened by existing within a framework of a renewed commitment to the cultural rights of citizens and communities.

We want a strategic move from arts policy to cultural policy.

We need a vision and language for the arts that includes a strong recognition of cultural rights, combined with actions which develop the creative and expressive lives of citizens and communities.

We argue for a vision of culture that connects our expressive lives with all aspects of the enrichment, health, security and development of civil society.

We urge a re-mix: let's find a new balance in the arts between the centre and the periphery, professional infrastructure and community capacity, our histories and our futures.

We encourage the direct involvement of civil society in the decision-making, the prioritising and distribution of the investment that supports the diversity of our creative and expressive lives.

We recognise that cultural participation builds the autonomy and protagonism of individuals and communities – we need policies that stimulate new models of dynamic citizenship.

Culture is our connector – invest in the flow. Let's ensure our cultural institutions function as porous spaces, engines of social and human transformation that can in turn be transformed.

We reaffirm the importance of international cultural exchange based on shared learning and creative collaboration, to ensure that the UK remains an evolving nation of diverse, shifting cultures – drawing inspiration and energy from outside ourselves.

Editors' acknowledgements

Our first thanks go to Célio Turino for providing the original inspiration with the *Cultura Viva* programme and his subsequent book *Ponto de Cultura*. We would like to acknowledge his generosity and his faith in allowing us to create this UK version of it. We are exceedingly grateful to Andrew Barnett, for his faith and vision in this project and to the Calouste Gulbenkian Foundation UK for helping to realise that vision in the publication of this book. Particular thanks must go to Felicity Luard for her gentle persistence and diligence in editing our new version of *The Point of Culture*, ably assisted by Oscar O'Sullivan.

The original book featured some arresting and beautiful images. We could not have gone ahead with this new version without the kind permission of TT Catalão, Nanan Catalão and Ratão Diniz to use their photographs here. Thanks also go to Emir Sader for allowing us to use and adapt his excellent original introduction; and to the Brazilian Embassy, for hosting a talk with Célio Turino in 2009 from which sprang a UK-Brazilian exchange programme and, ultimately, this book. Gratitude is due too to Thiago Jesus and Sara Kewly Hyde at People's Palace Projects for their support and encouragement in bringing this to fruition.

None of our work on the *Points of Contact* programme would be possible without the generous financial and thinking support of Arts Council England, the British Council, the Department for Culture, Media and Sport, and Queen Mary University of London, in the UK and from the Ministry of Culture, FUNARTE, Rio de Janeiro State Culture Secretariat and Petrobras in Brazil.

And, finally, our heart-felt thanks to all the artists from *Pontos/ Points of Culture* in Brazil and the UK whose experiences have inspired us to bring this into being. We salute you.

Appreciation and *abraços*

Paul Heritage, Rosie Hunter and Poppy Spowage

Biographies

Célio Turino Historian, writer, politician and cultural policy maker, Célio Turino was Secretary of Cultural Citizenship for Brazil's Ministry of Culture from 2004–10 and the architect of *Cultura Viva*. Turino was responsible for creating and implementing the *Ponto de Cultura* programme which today reaches over 8 million people via 3,000 points spread all over Brazil. This radical socio-cultural programme has become a highly influential reference for public policy in several countries across Latin America.

Célio Turino holds a BA and MA in History from UNICAMP (Universidade Estadual de Campinas) and a MBA in Cultural Administration from PUC-SP (Pontifícia Universidade Católica de São Paulo). His public positions have included Secretary of Culture, city of Campinas (one million inhabitants), state of São Paulo, 1990-2; Director of Sports and Leisure, city of São Paulo (20 million inhabitants), 2001–4. His published books include *Na trilha de Macunaíma: Ócio e trabalho na cidade* (On the trail of Macunaíma: Leisure and work in the city), SENAC, São Paulo (2005), and *Ponto de Cultura: o Brasil de baixo para cima* (The Point of Culture: Brazil turned upside down), Anita Garibaldi, São Paulo (2009; 2nd edn 2010).

Paul Heritage is Professor of Drama and Performance at Queen Mary University of London, and Director of People's Palace Projects. In 2004, he was made a Knight of the Order of the Rio Branco by the Brazilian government in recognition of his services to Anglo-Brazilian cultural relations. He co-founded the Theatre in Prisons (TIPP) Centre in England and for fifteen years has directed theatre-based human rights projects in prisons across twelve states in Brazil. As a producer he has worked with some of the UK's leading arts institutions to bring a range of Brazilian artists to British audiences, including *Grupo Galpão* (Shakespeare's Globe Theatre), *Grupo Piollin* (Barbican), *AfroReggae* (Barbican/Southbank Centre/Contact Theatre/Liverpool Everyman and Playhouse/Salisbury Festival) and *Nós do Morro* (Royal Shakespeare Company). As International Associate at the Young Vic Theatre, he directed a sequence of performances, debates and workshops linked to popular culture in the Amazon region of Brazil. Paul Heritage has directed Shakespeare in some of Rio de Janeiro's most distinguished theatres as well as on the borderlands of conflict in the *favelas* of Vigário Geral, Parada de Lucas, Rocinha, etc. In association with fifteen venues across London, Heritage and the People's Palace Projects team produced *Rio Occupation London*, bringing thirty Rio artists for a thirty-day creative occupation during London 2012 Festival. Author of a number of publications about Brazil, he has a studio theatre named after him in the maximum security prison of Brasília.

Rosie Hunter is Executive Director and **Poppy Spowage** is Projects Manager of **People's Palace Projects**, an independent arts charity based at Queen Mary University of London, that conducts research to advance the practice and understanding of art for social justice. Under Paul Heritage's direction, it has spent the last seventeen years creating and debating art that makes a difference to people's lives. From Rio to London, Liverpool to Azerbaijan, its creative projects and cultural exchange programmes have sought out contexts where art matters most, with a special focus on strengthening cultural links between Brazil and the UK.

PPP has active partnerships with a range of arts organisations and artists across England, Wales, Scotland and Northern Ireland, and a legacy of international collaborative projects in West Africa, South America and Eastern Europe. PPP is a National Portfolio Organisation of Arts Council England. For further information see www.peoplespalace.org.uk